Halloween Coloring Book

by

Kitty Belle

Copyright © 2020 Kitty Belle

HALLOWEEN COLORING BOOK

BY

KITTY BELLE

WARNING - CONTENTS ARE SCARY AS HELL!

COLOR IN AT YOUR OWN RISK!

Halloween Coloring Book Intro

Hello, you horrible little rat bags. Well, what do we have here then? Come here for some scary coloring have you then? Want to bring to life the horrors and ghouls from Halloween? Well, you're in the right place for a super scary Halloween ride straight to hell!

So, perhaps on a more serious note, I should welcome you properly to this terrifying and utterly gruesome coloring book filled with ghastly ghouls, creepy critters, half-dead zombies (okay, they're probably fully dead really), wicked witches, skinny skeletons and fiendish fairies (you might find a couple of nicer ones too if you're lucky).

Halloween is one of the most fun events of the year where we can all get dressed up in our frighteningly scary costumes to terrorize our neighborhoods in exchange for delicious candy. It's a tradition that's been round for years. The word 'Halloween' actually dates back to around the mid eighteenth century and comes from the Scottish term for All Hallows' Eve - the evening before All Hallows' Day. From this, 'eve' gets shortened to 'een' or 'e'en' and then becomes 'Halloween'. Who knew Halloween could be so interesting right?

So, what about coloring? Well, it's a well-known fact that decompartmentalizing and stepping away from the trials and tribulations of daily life is hugely important in today's society. There's so much stuff for us to think and worry about; schools, work, money, relationships... it all adds up. So, why not just put all that to one side, get your jack-o-lanterns at the ready, stick on some freakishly scary music and get bring to life the super scary illustrations that feature in this book. Be careful though as some of them are pretty, well, scary!

You can bring to life these super-scary illustrations with whichever mediums you wish. You may choose to go for some grey scale shading for a truly dark and sinister finish. You could choose bright vibrant colors to bring out the blood and gore that graces the pages of this book. Either way, you should have a whole lot of fun along the way.

Just be careful and remember.... Enter only at your own risk...

Muhahahahahahahahaha....

Over and out,

Kitty B

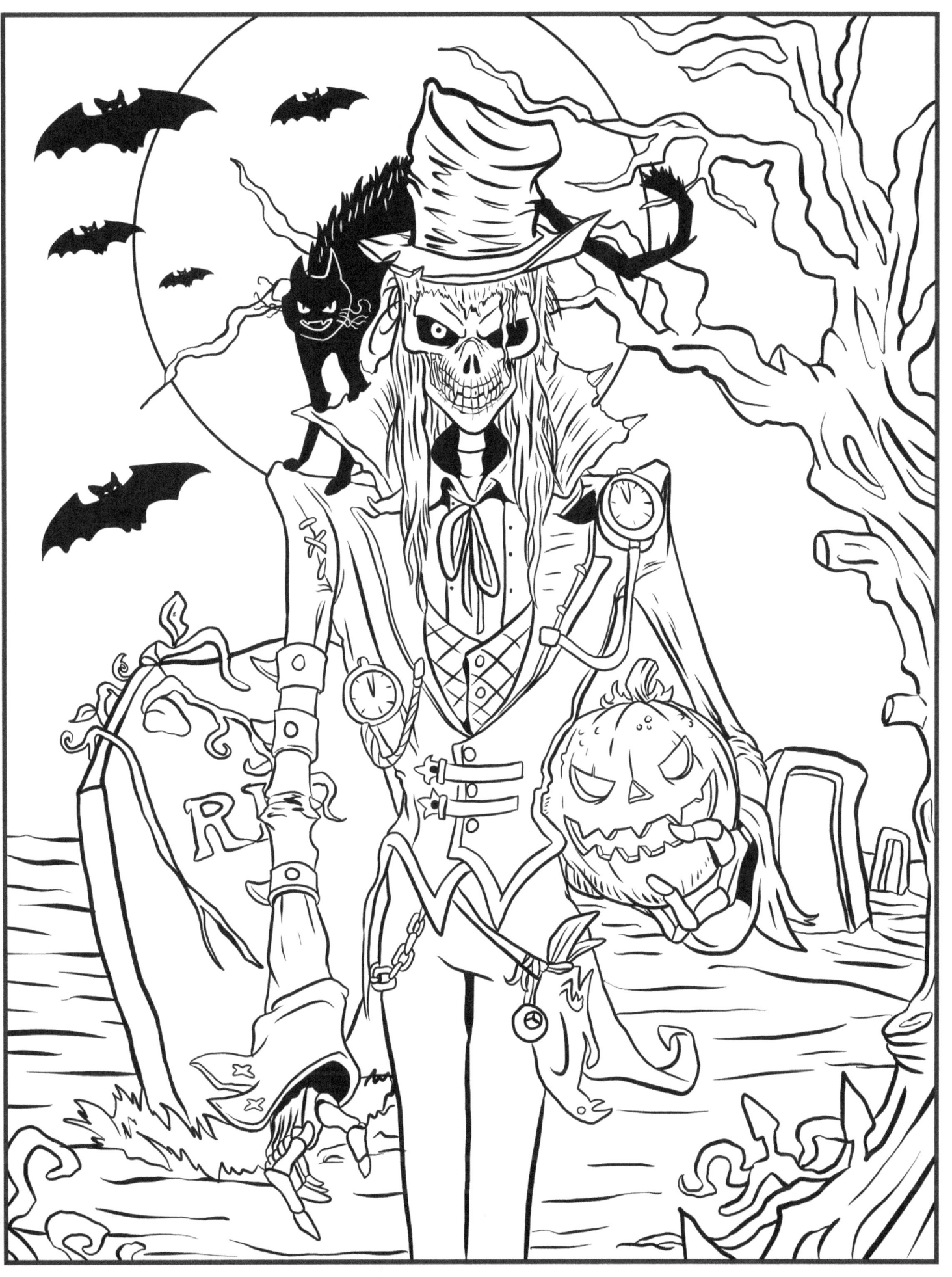

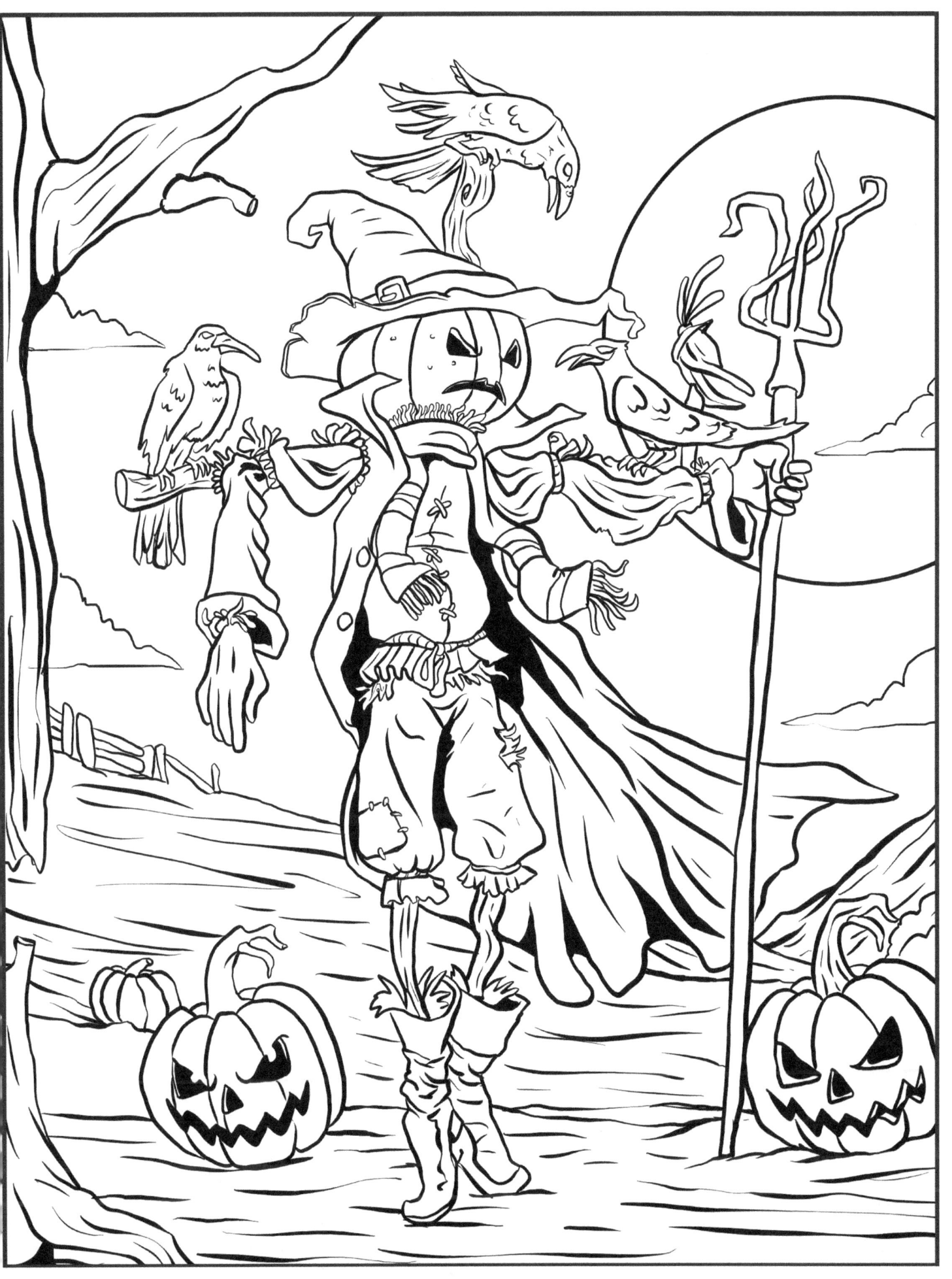

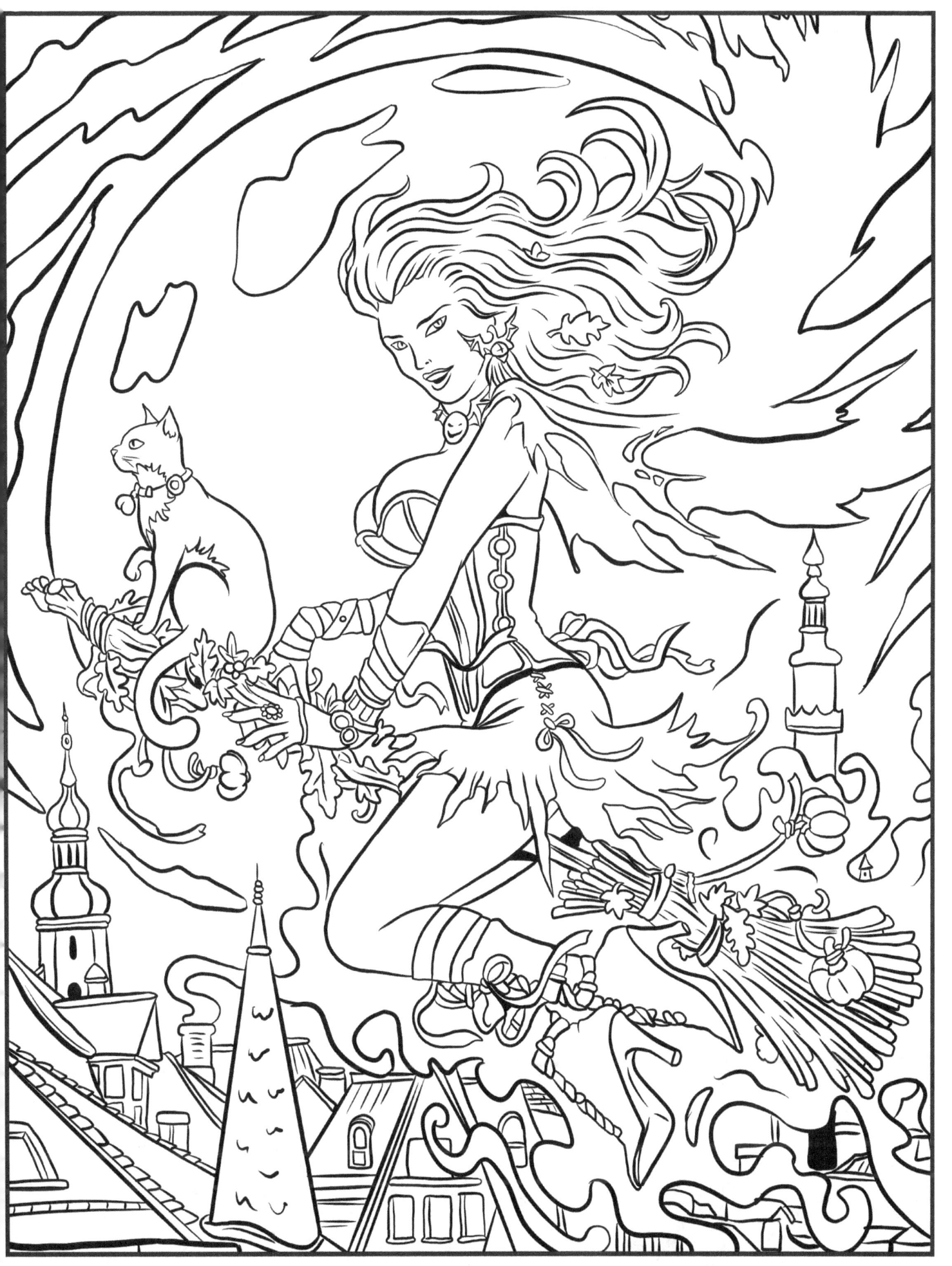

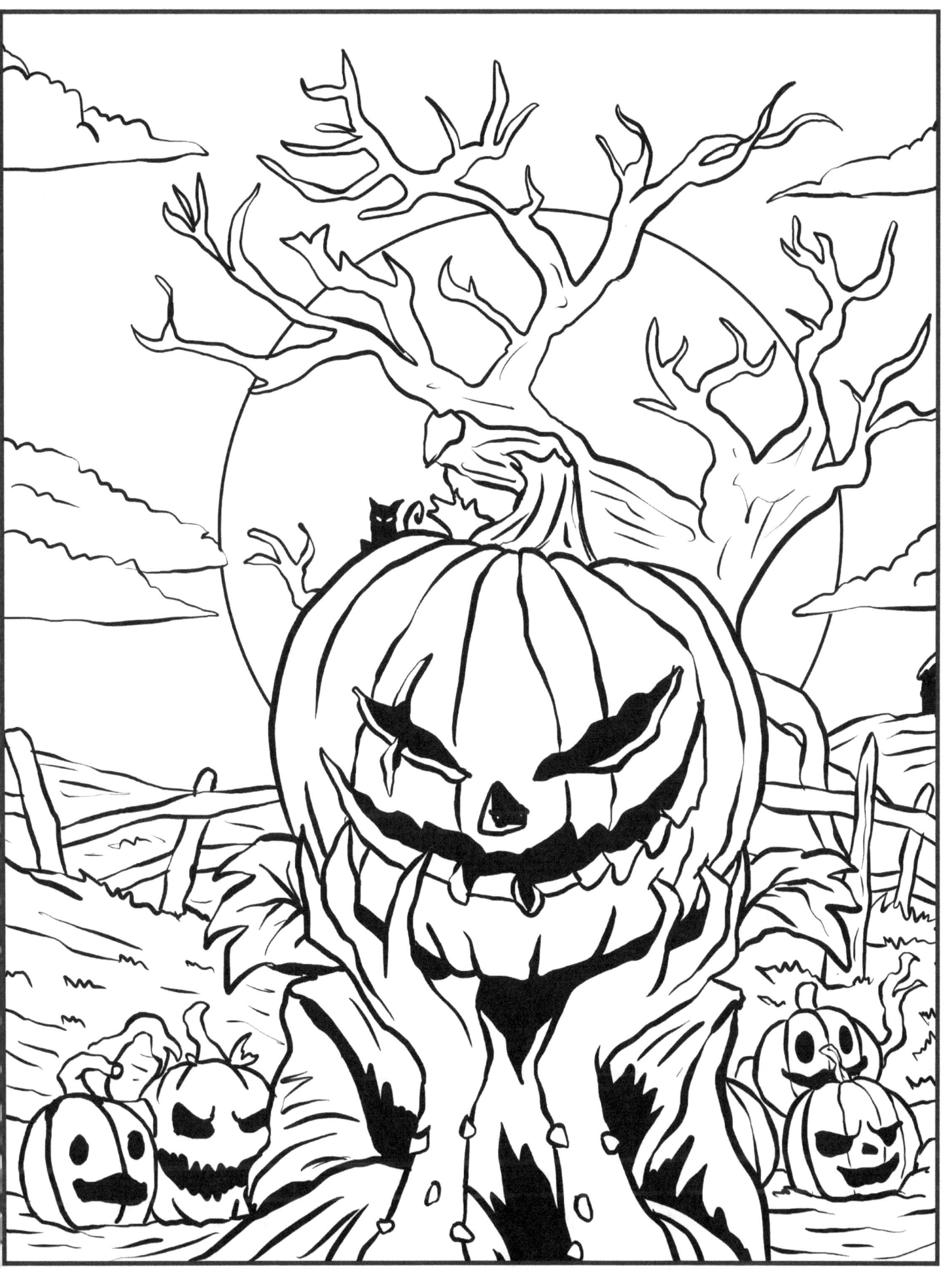

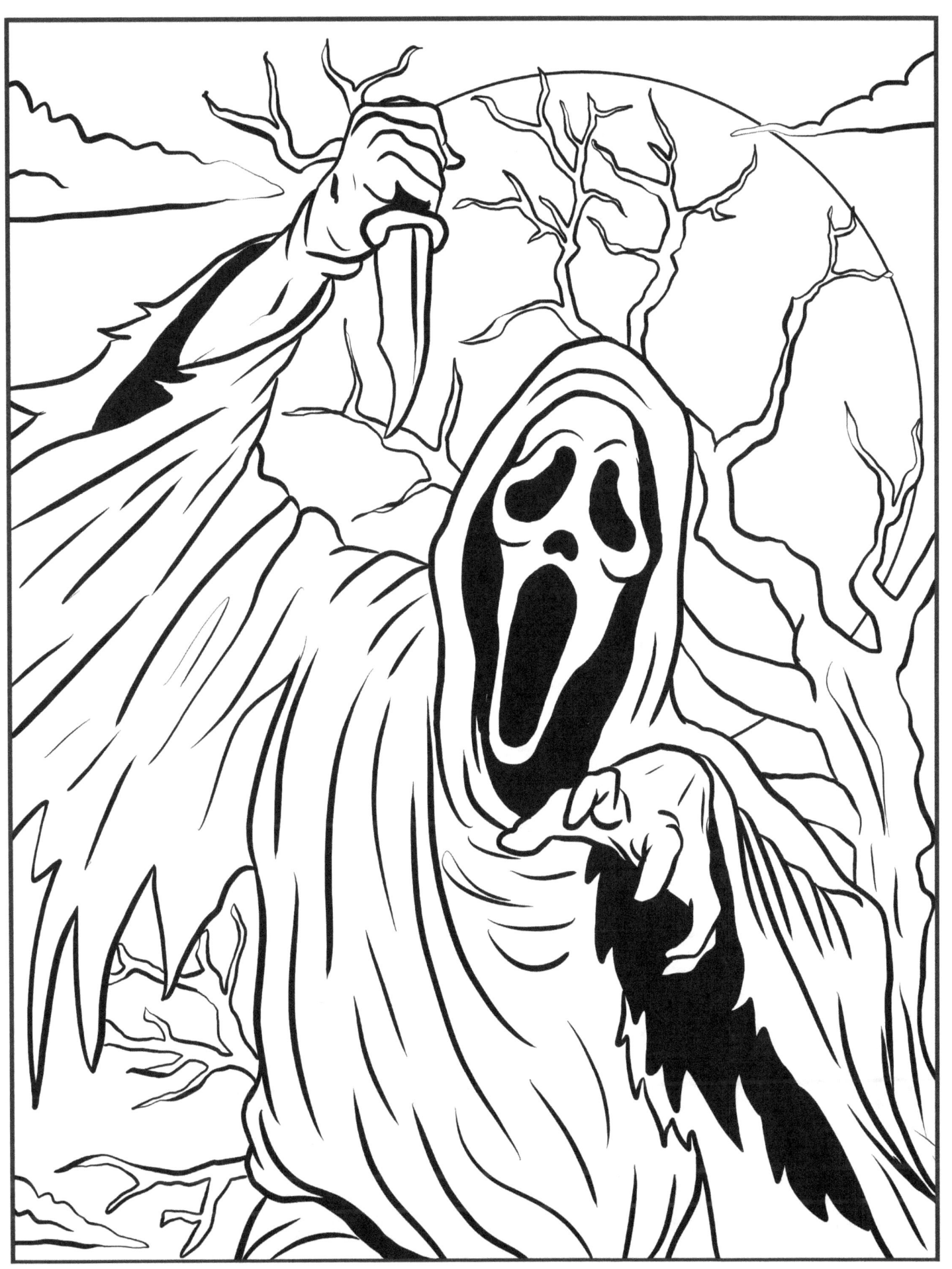

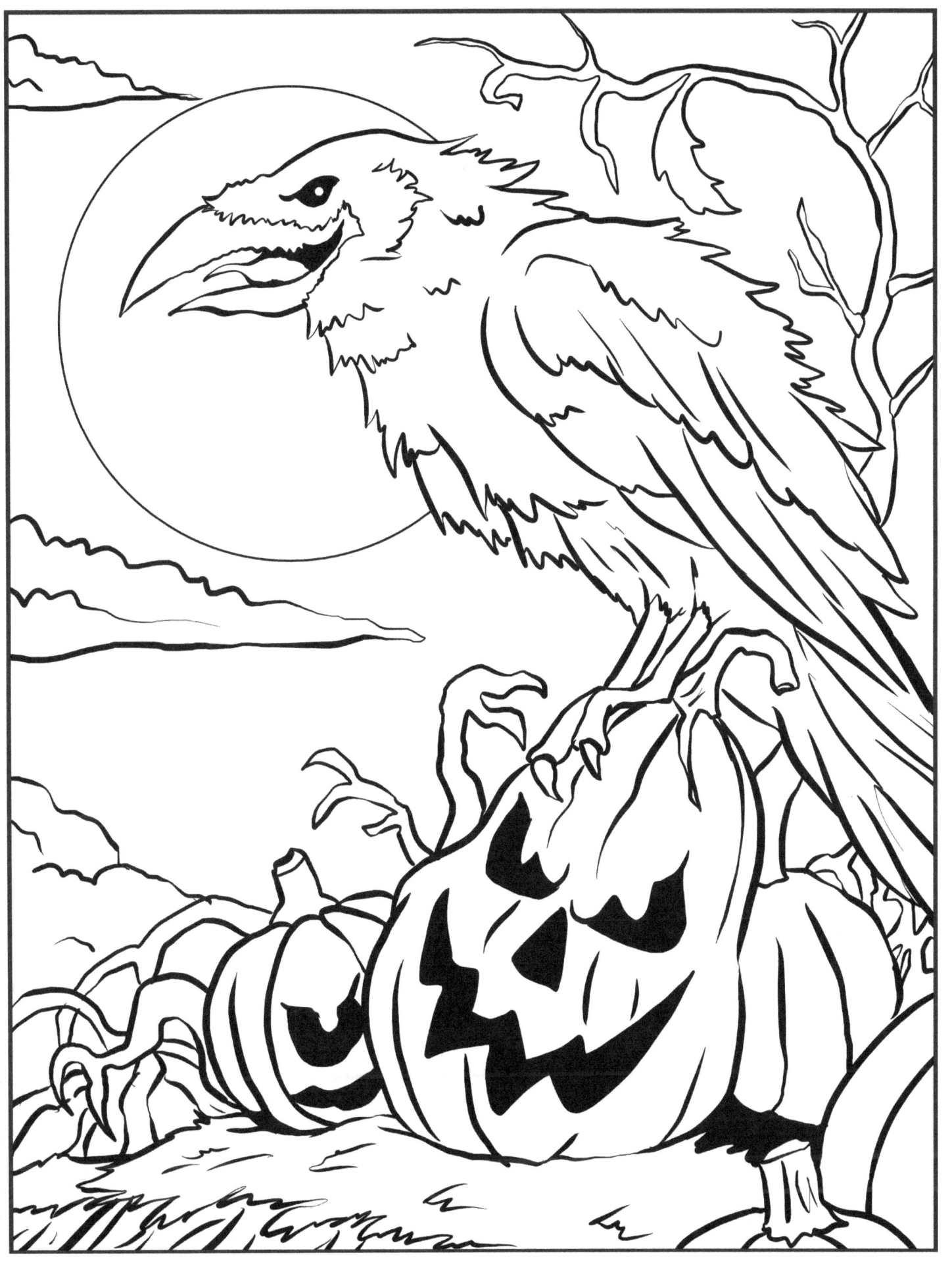

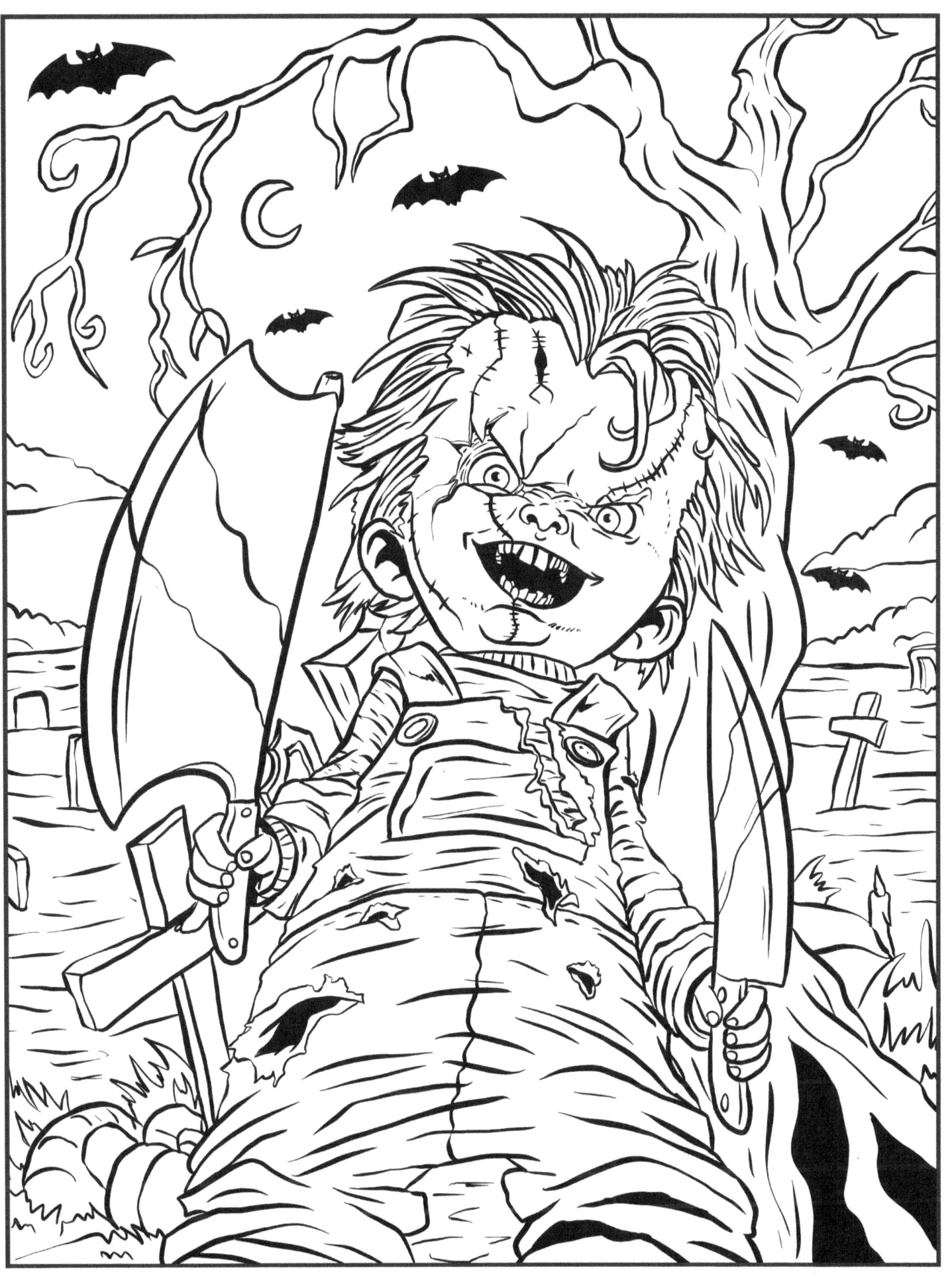

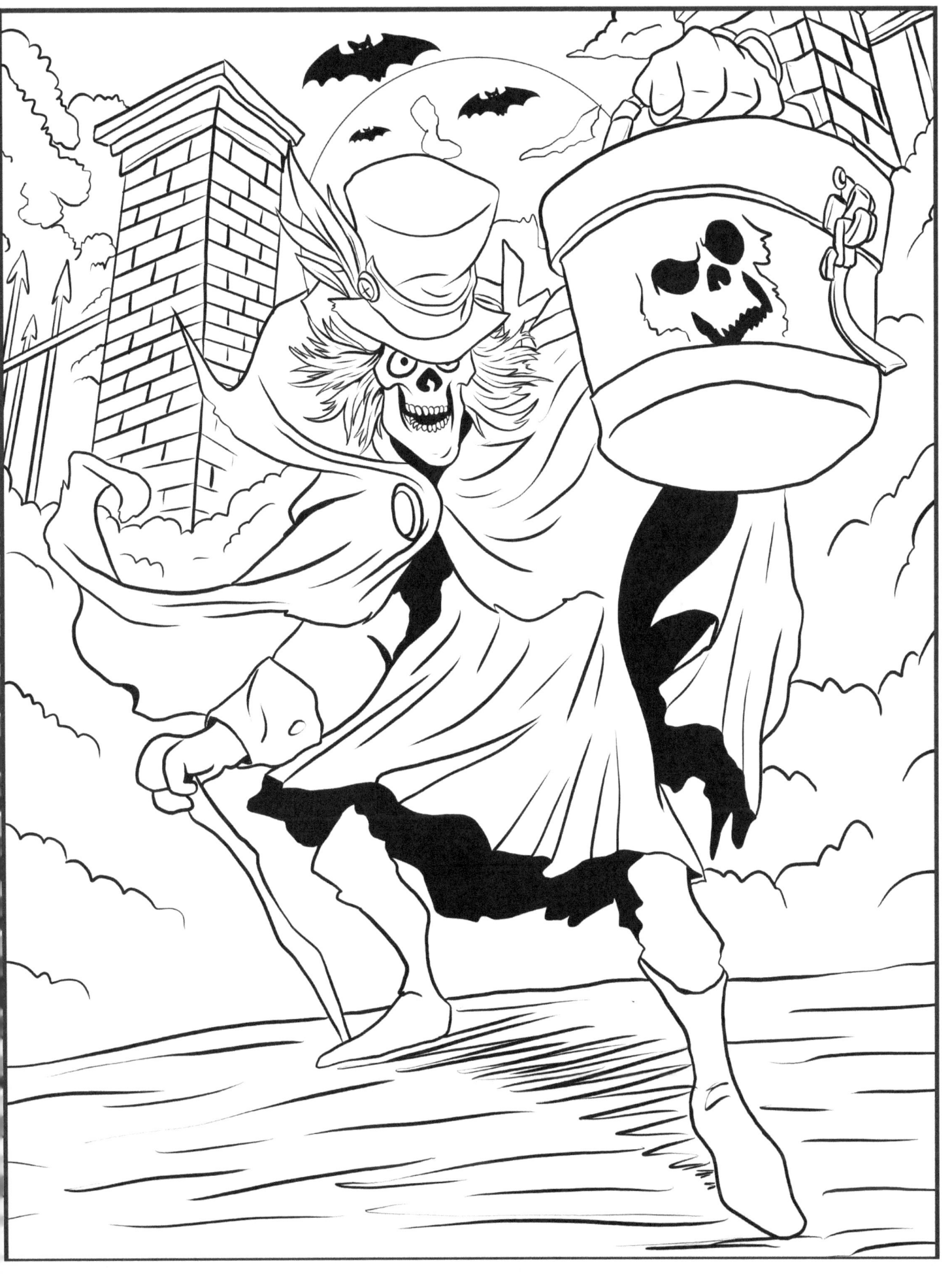

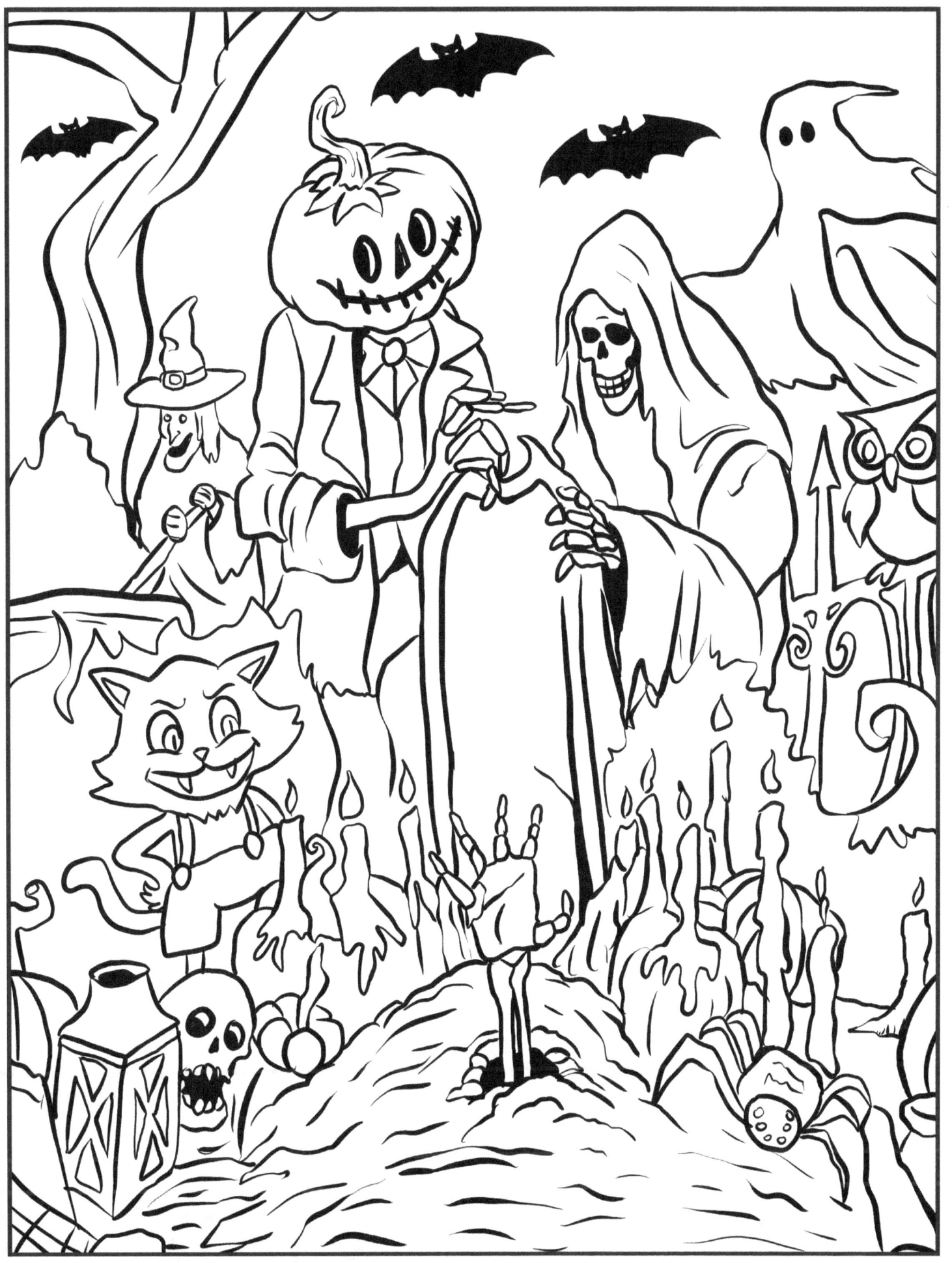

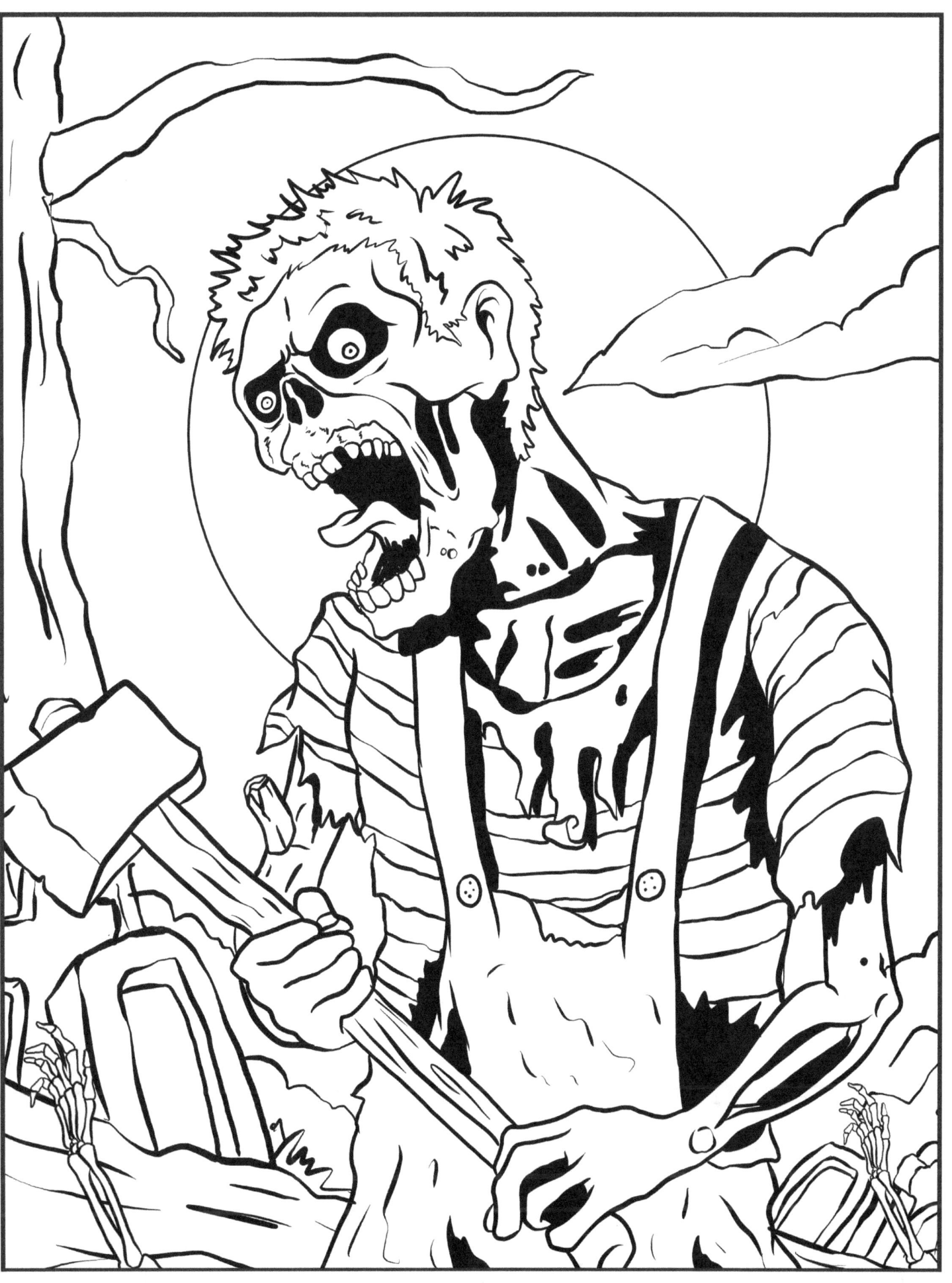

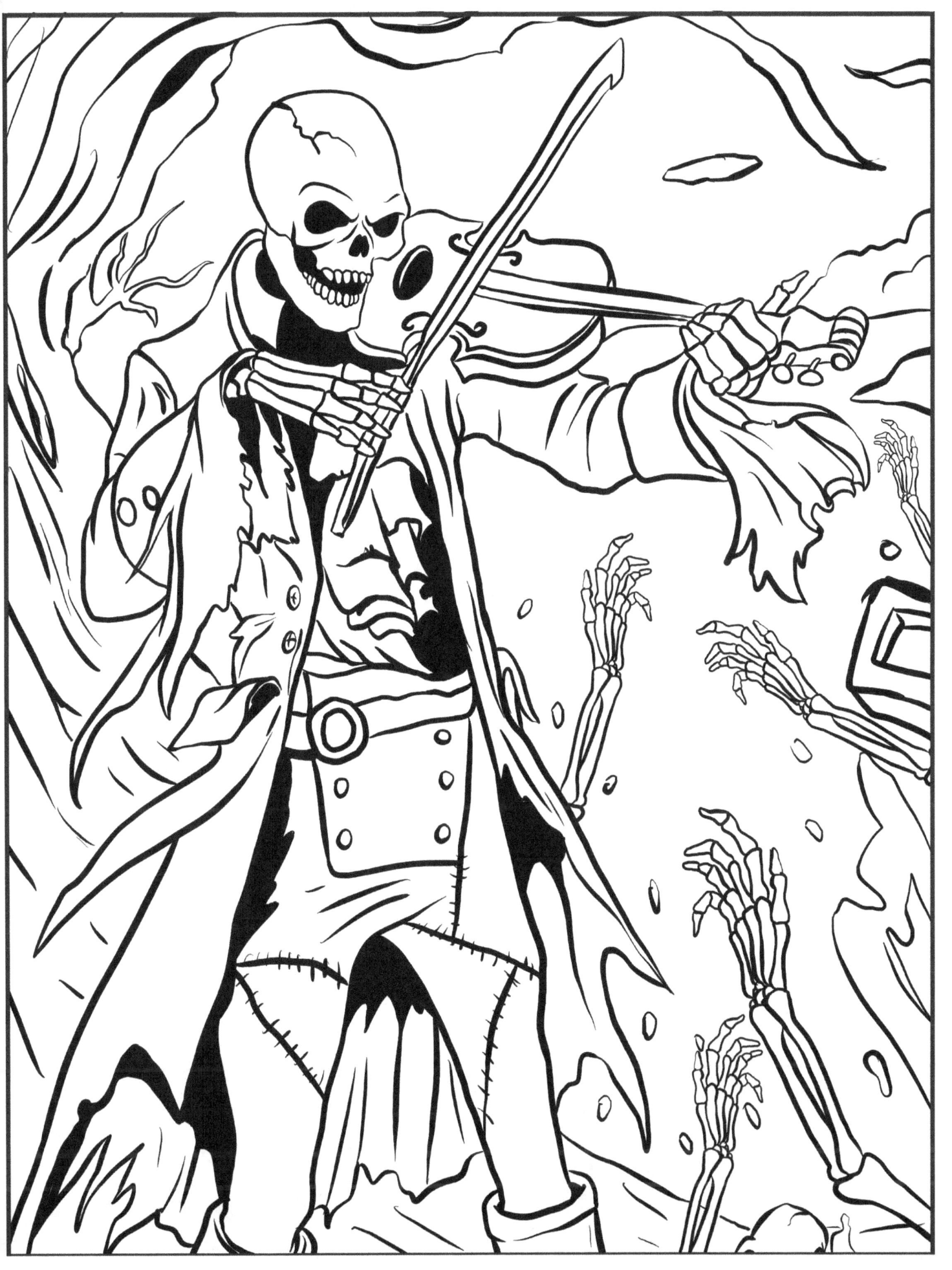

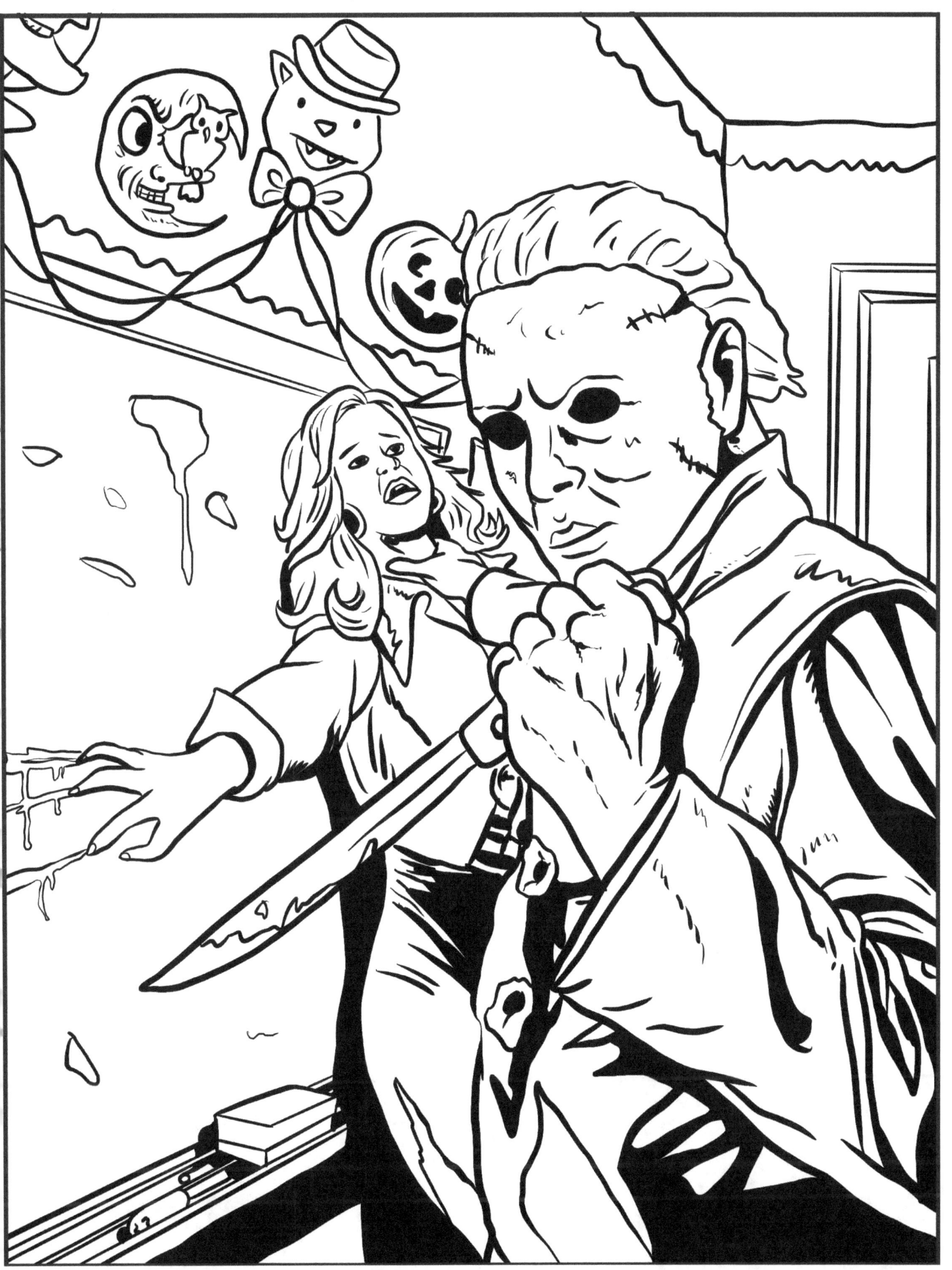

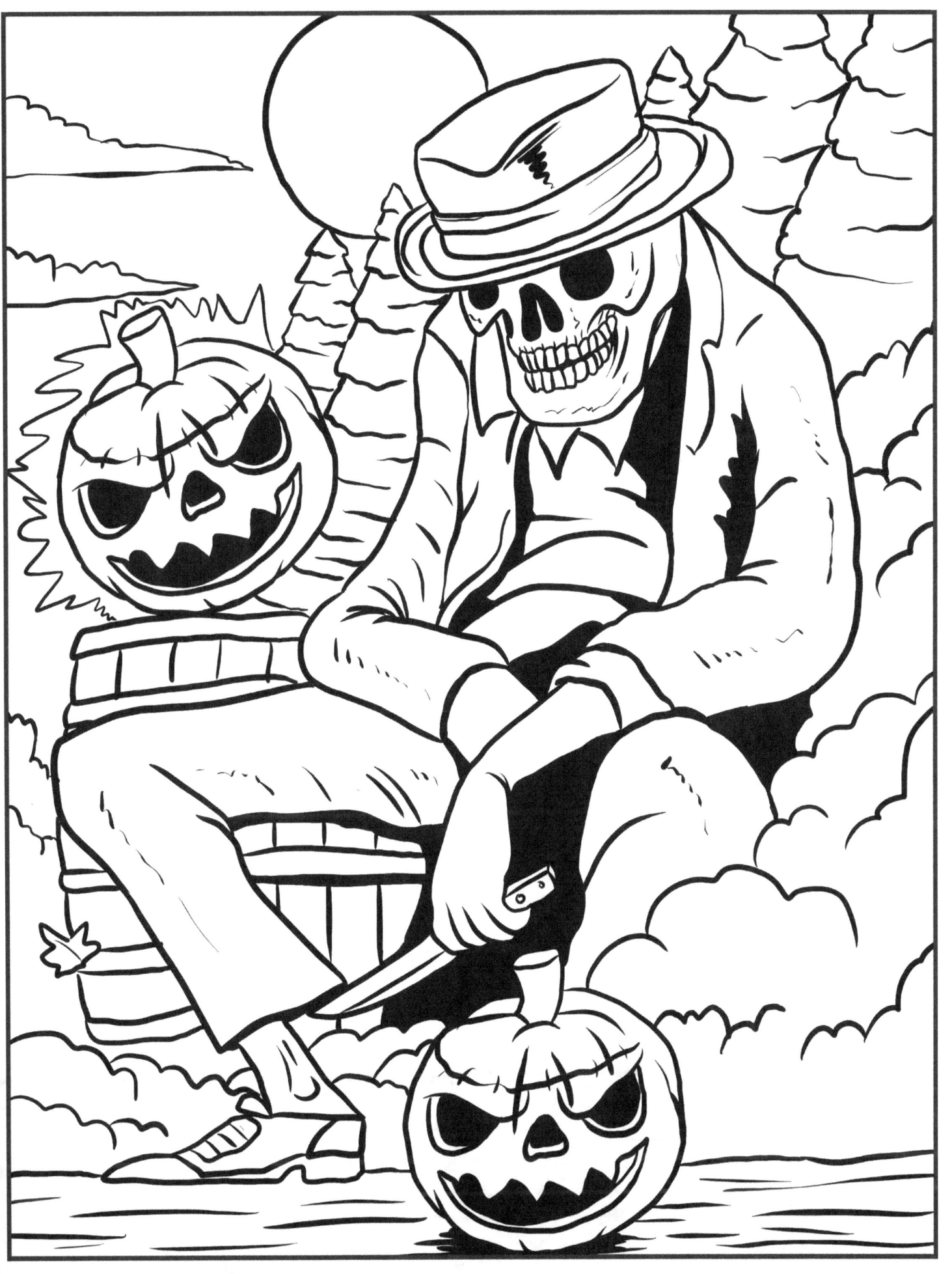

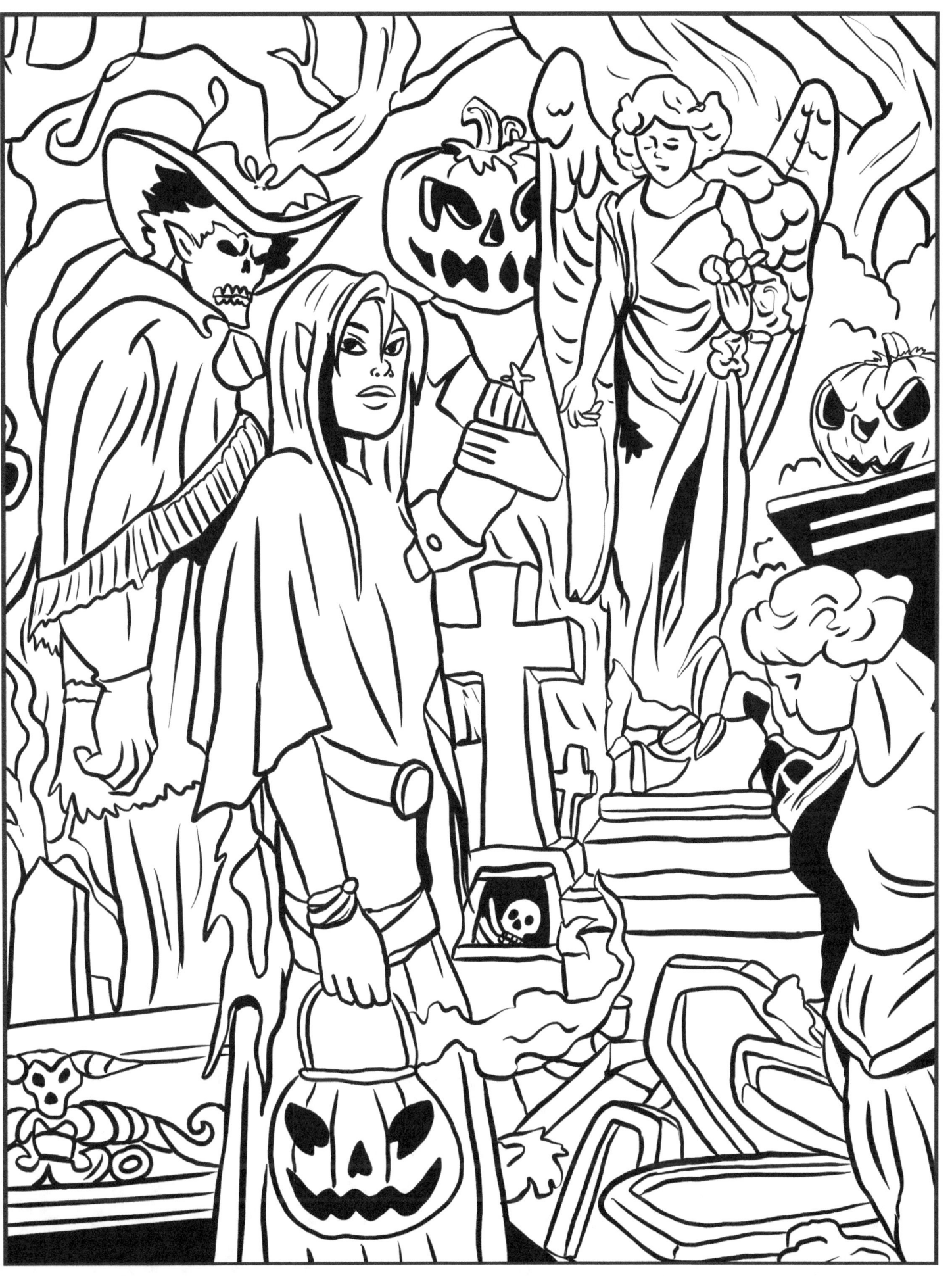

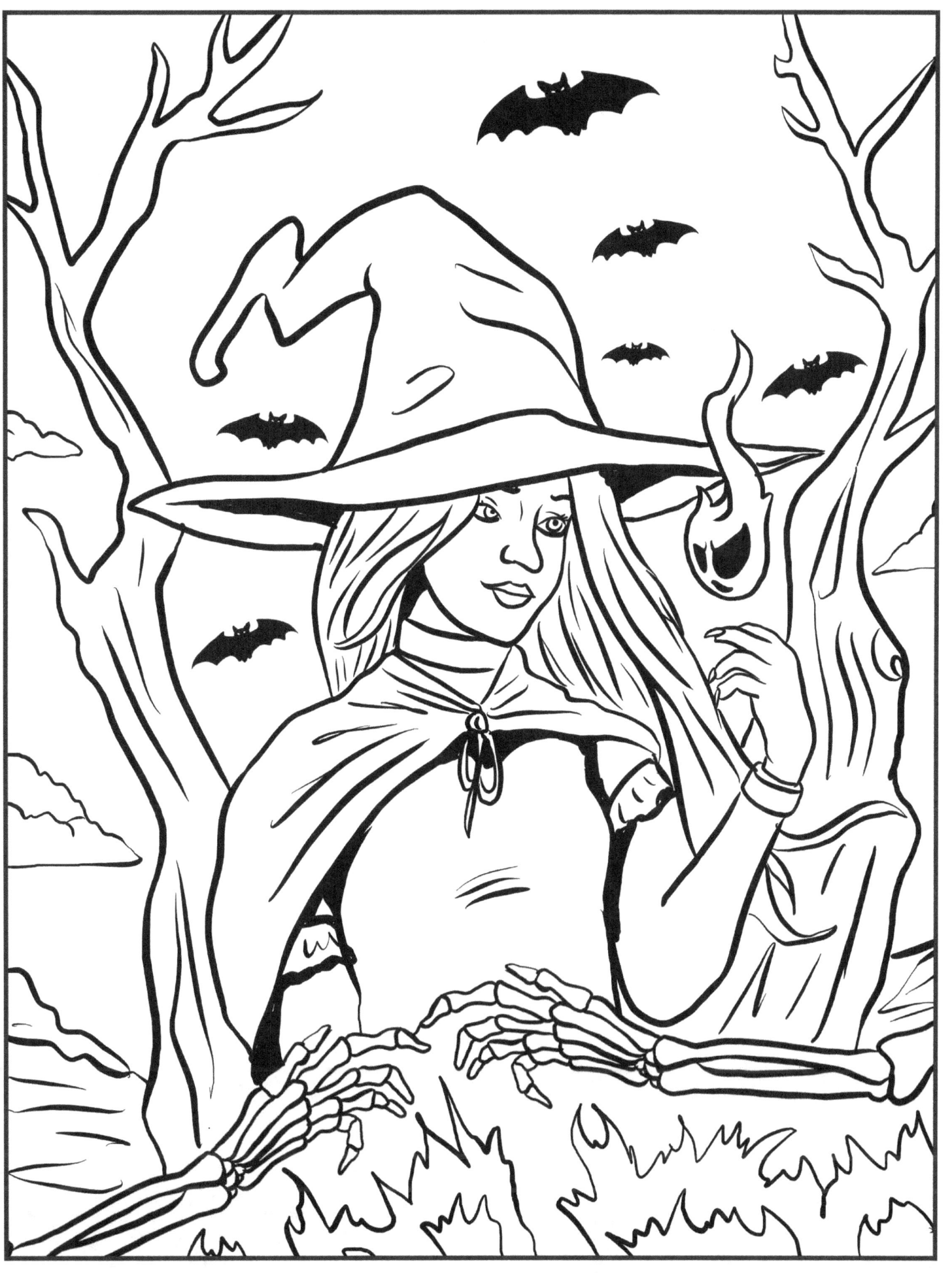

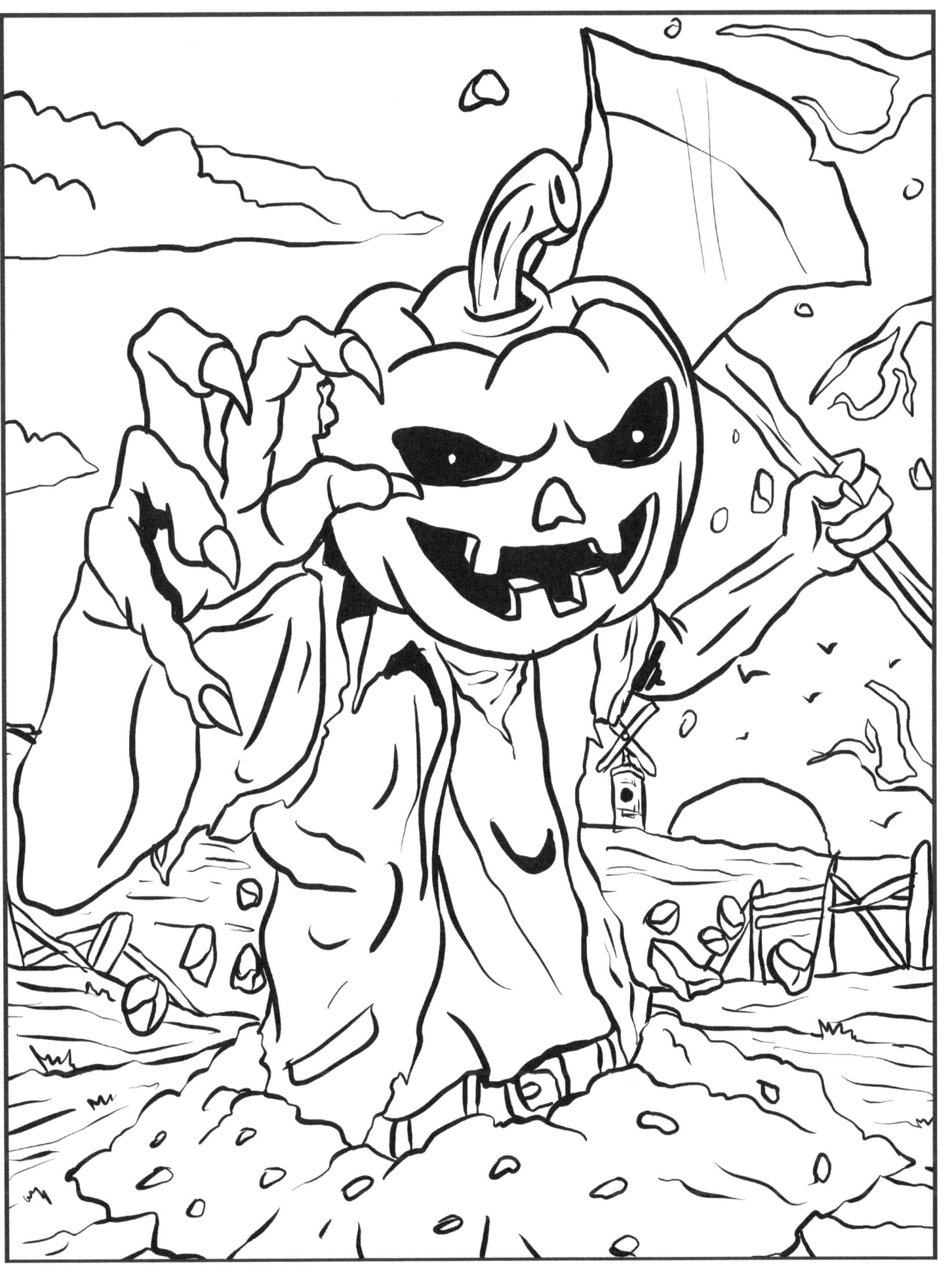

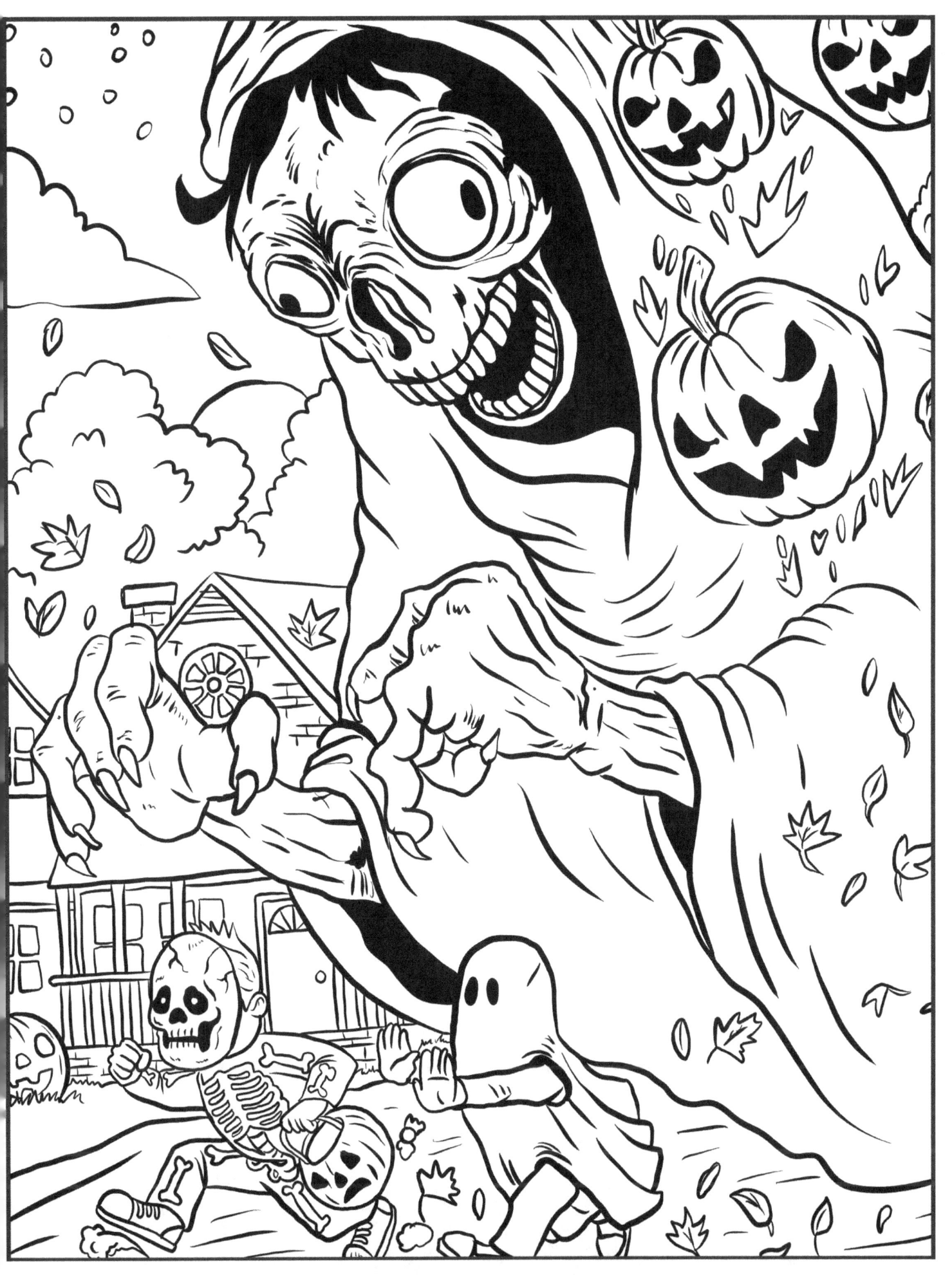

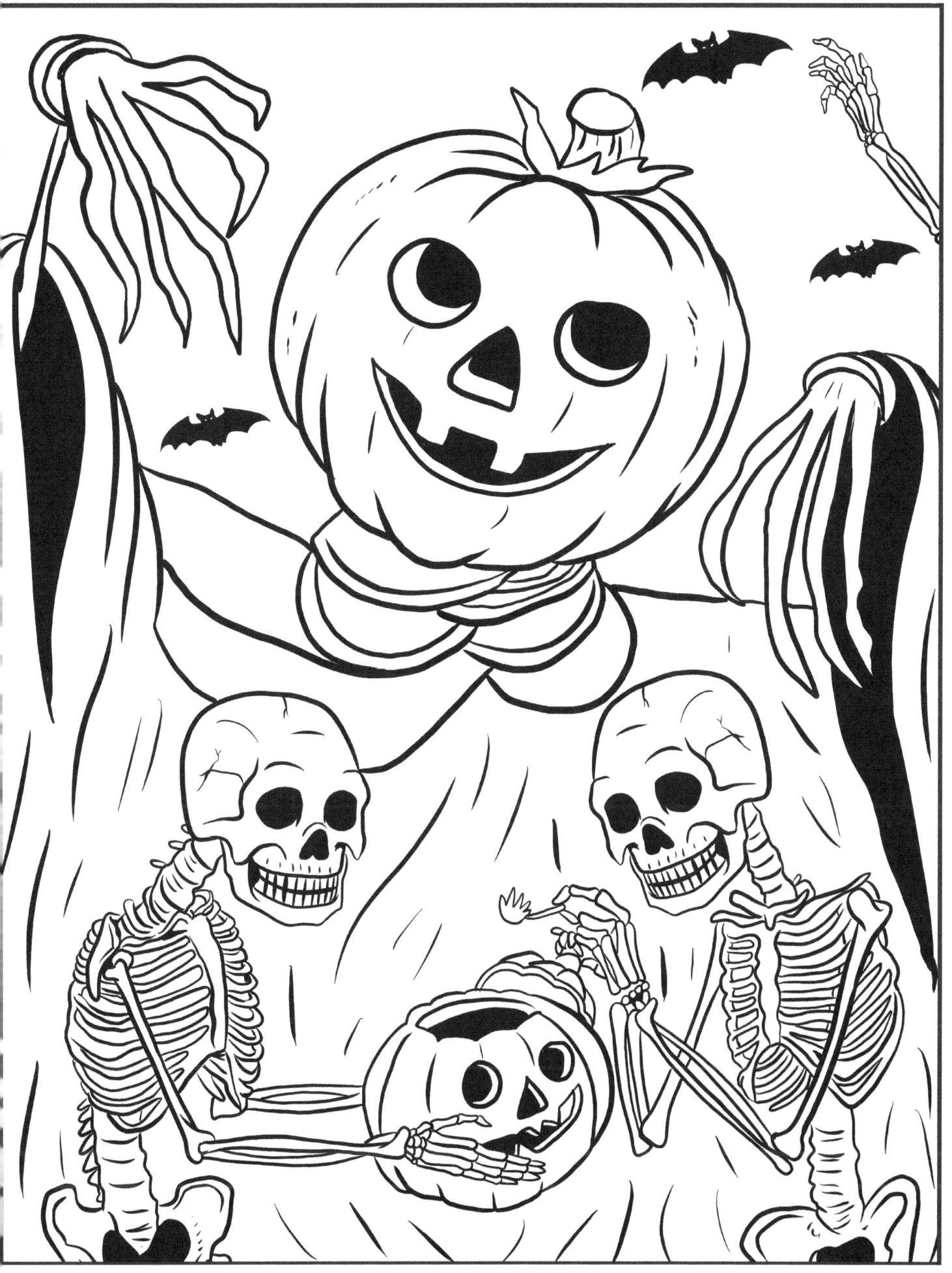

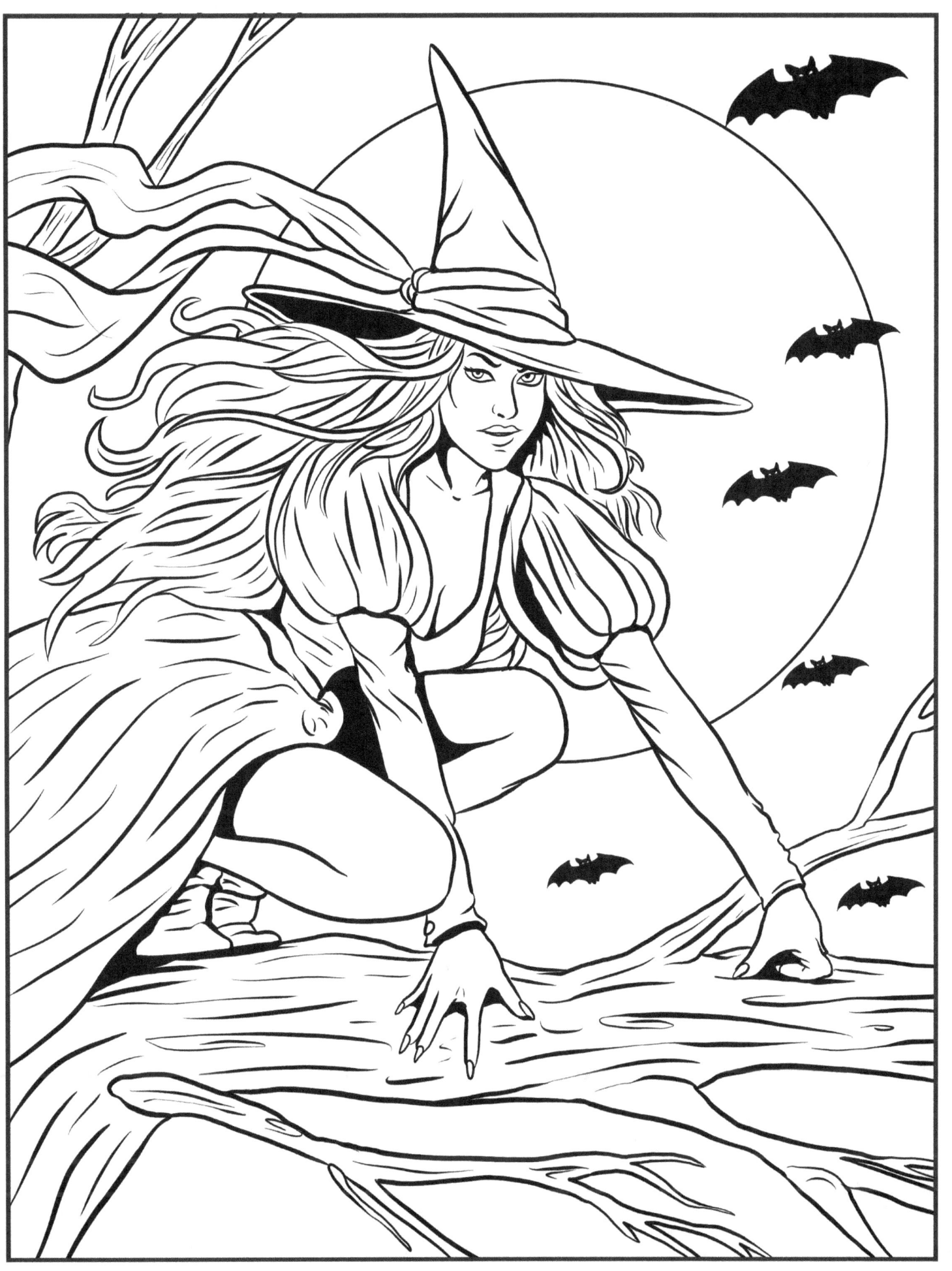

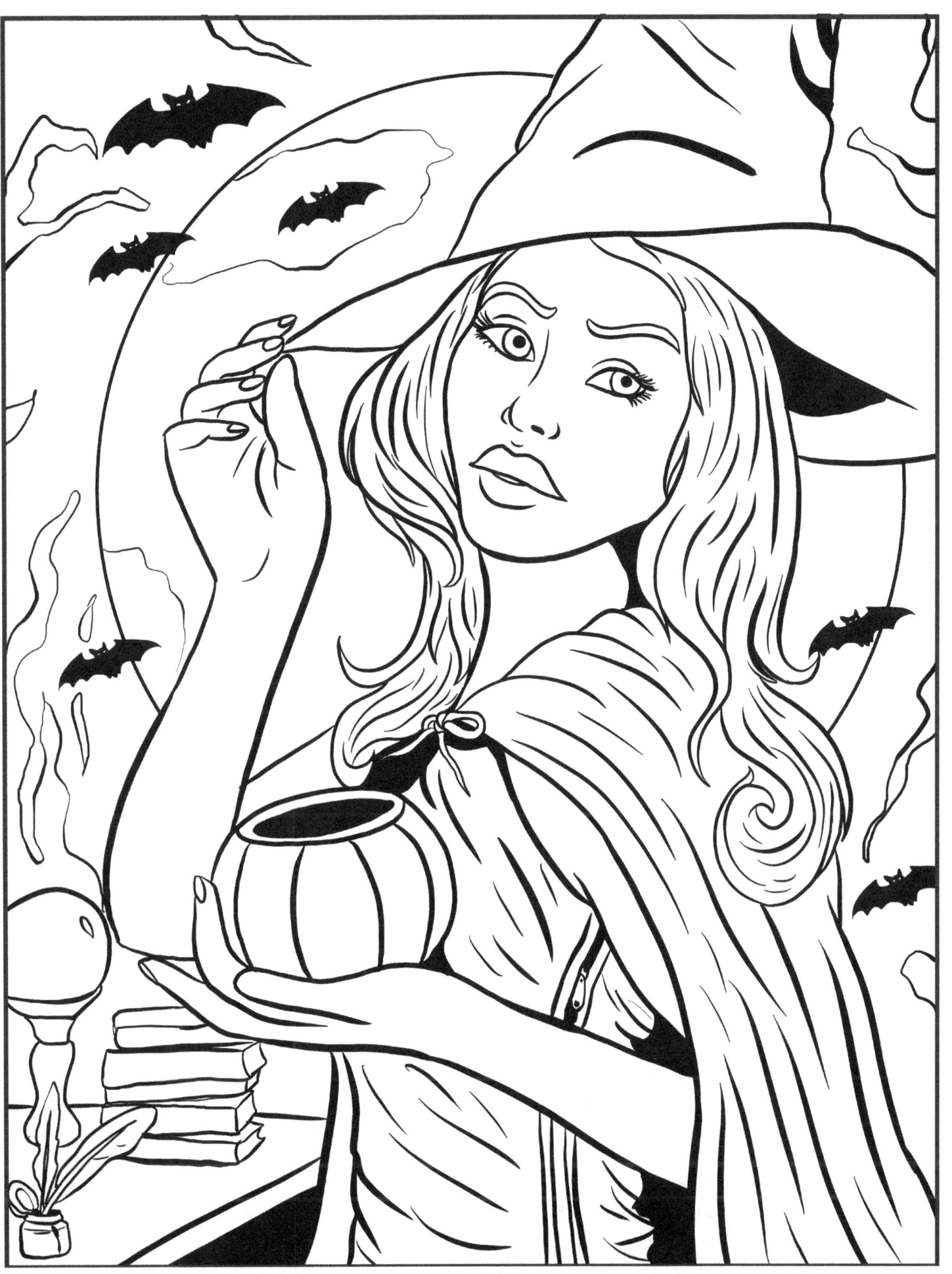

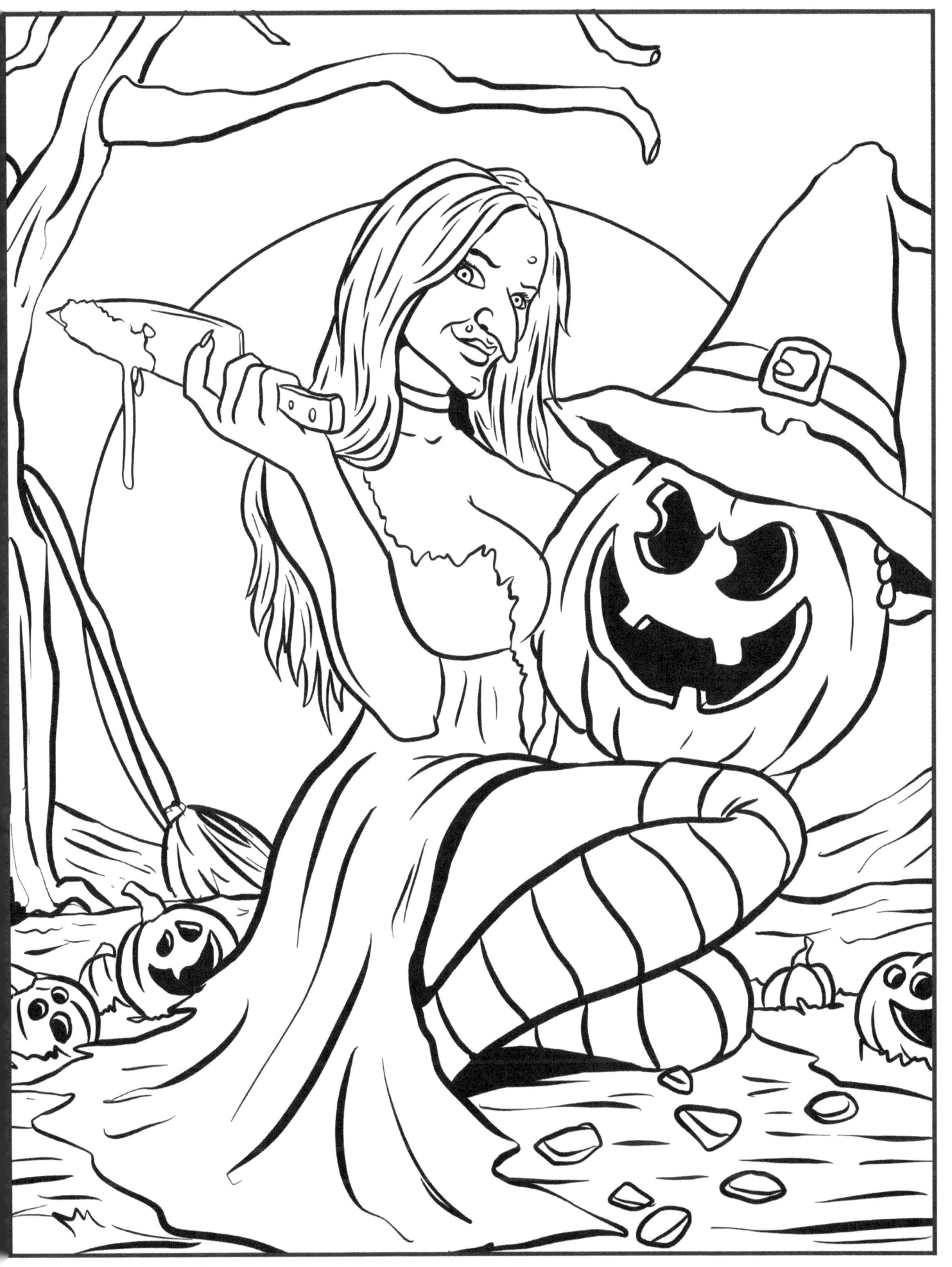

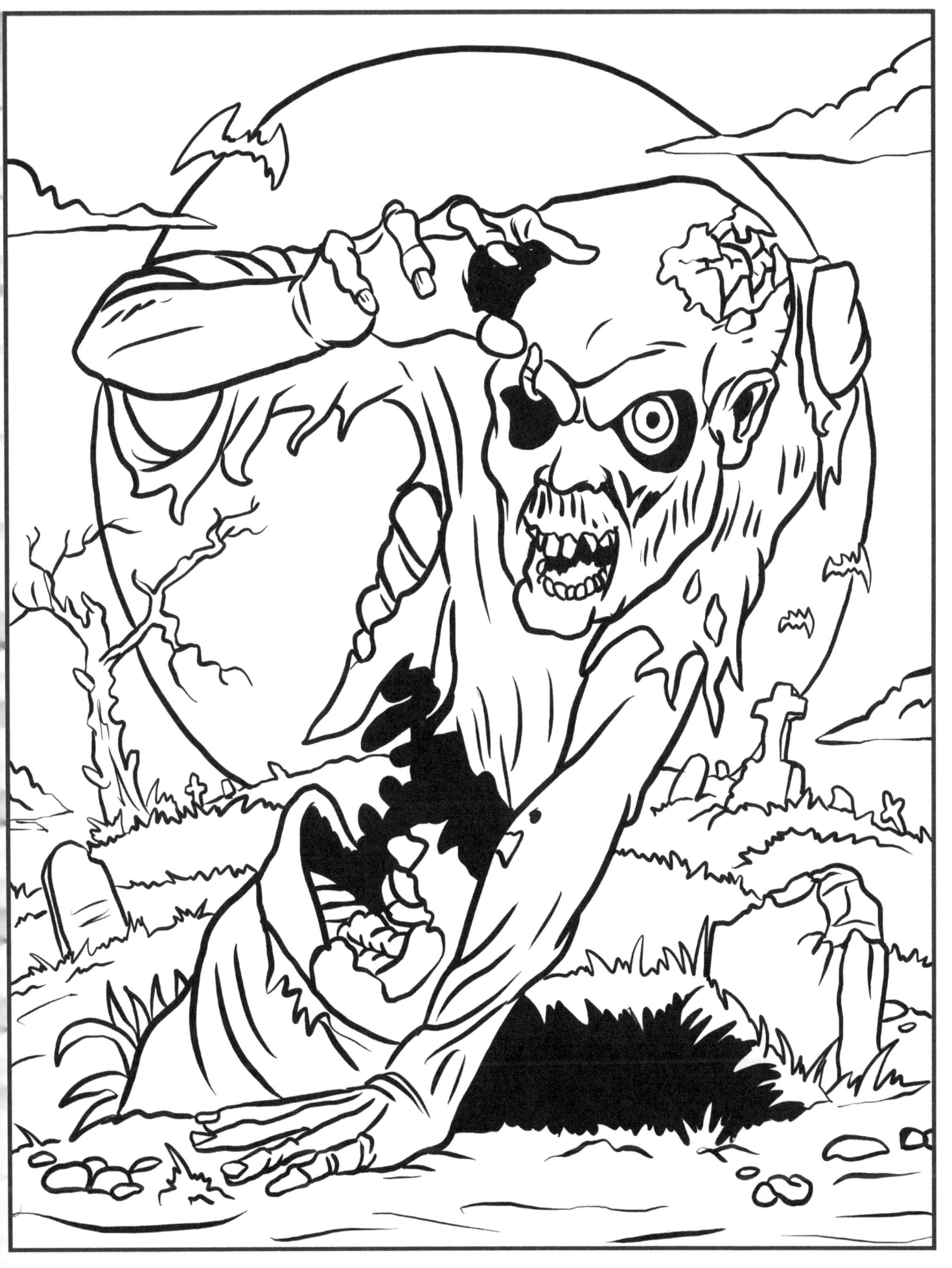

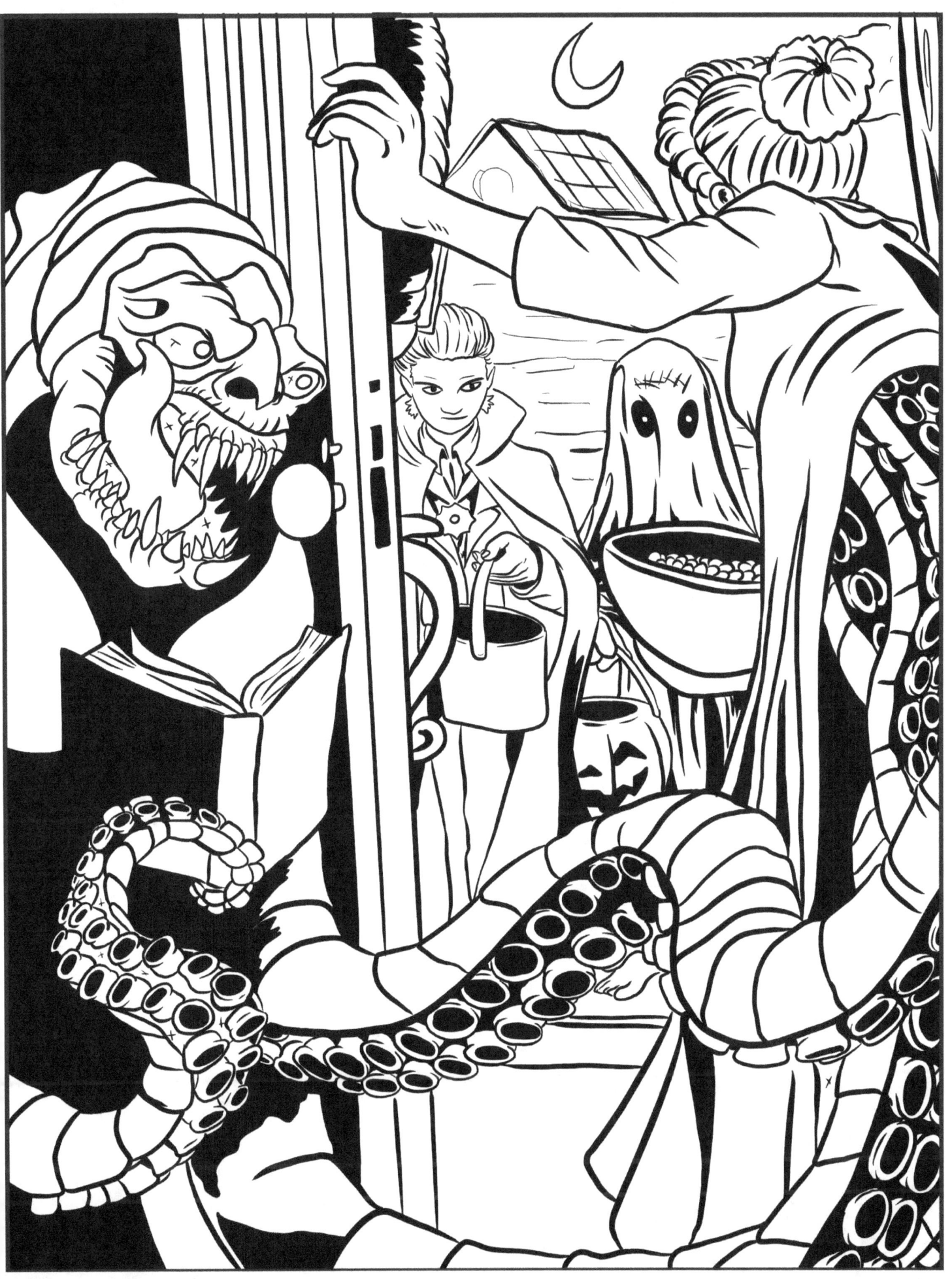

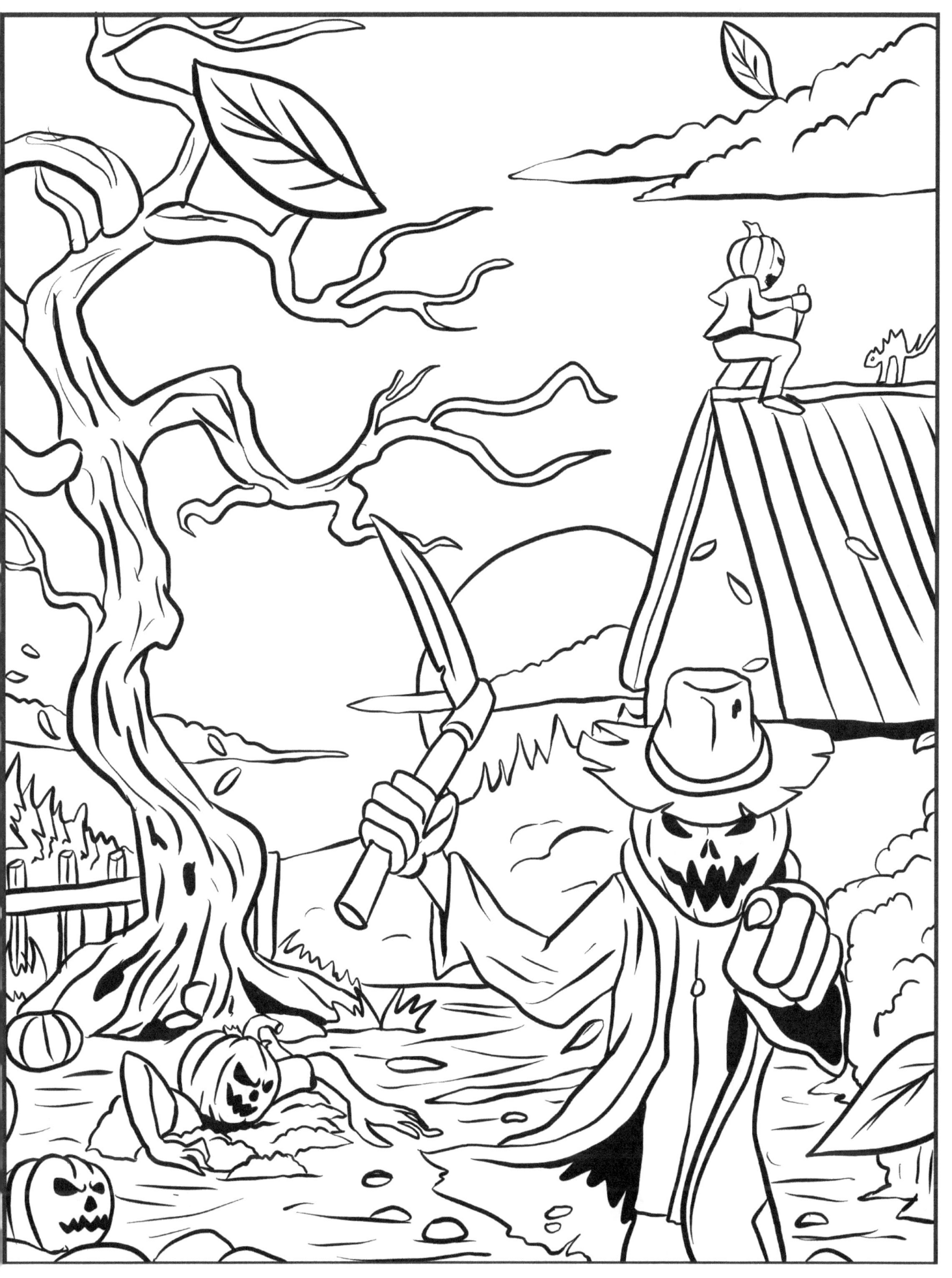

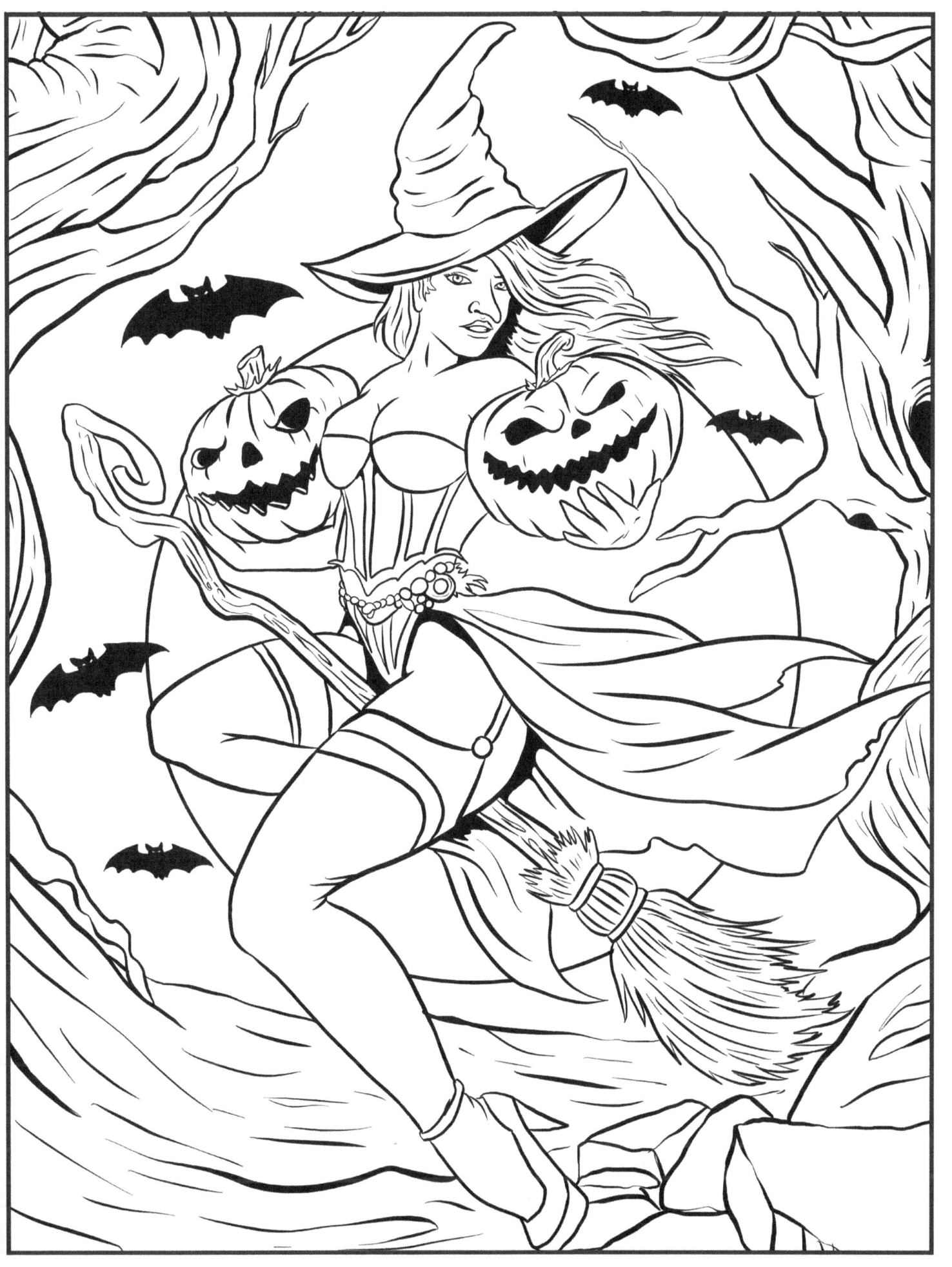

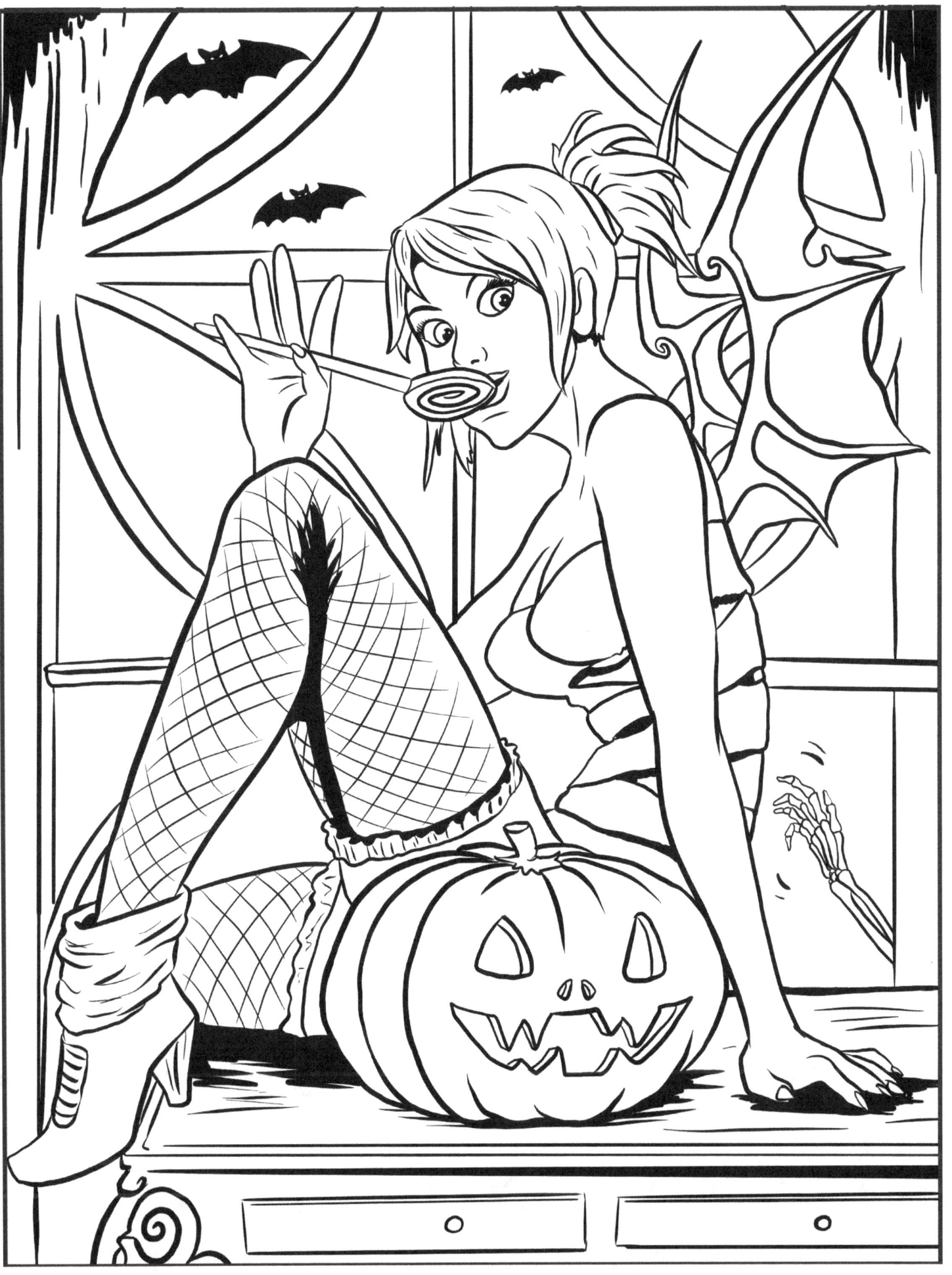

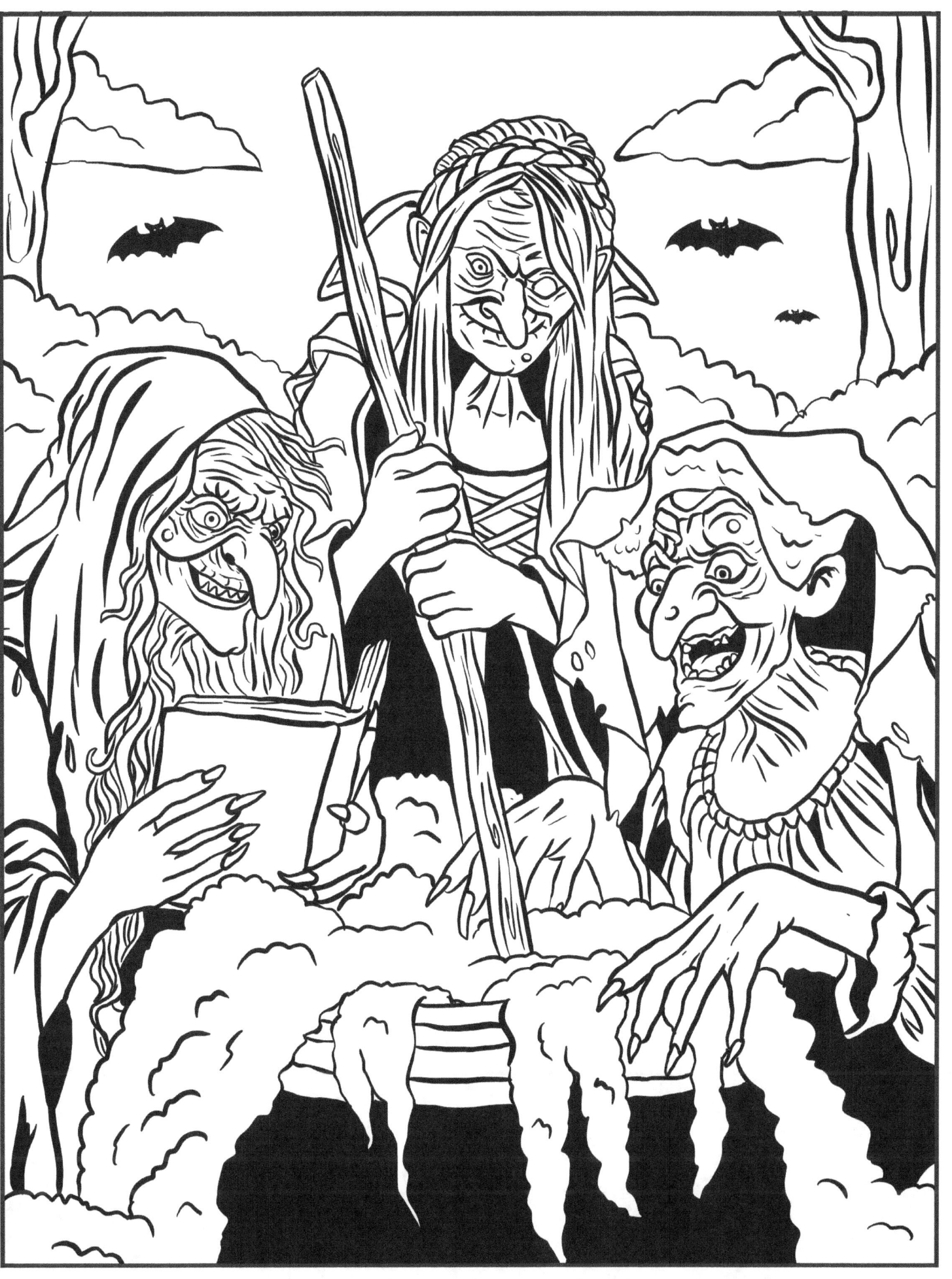

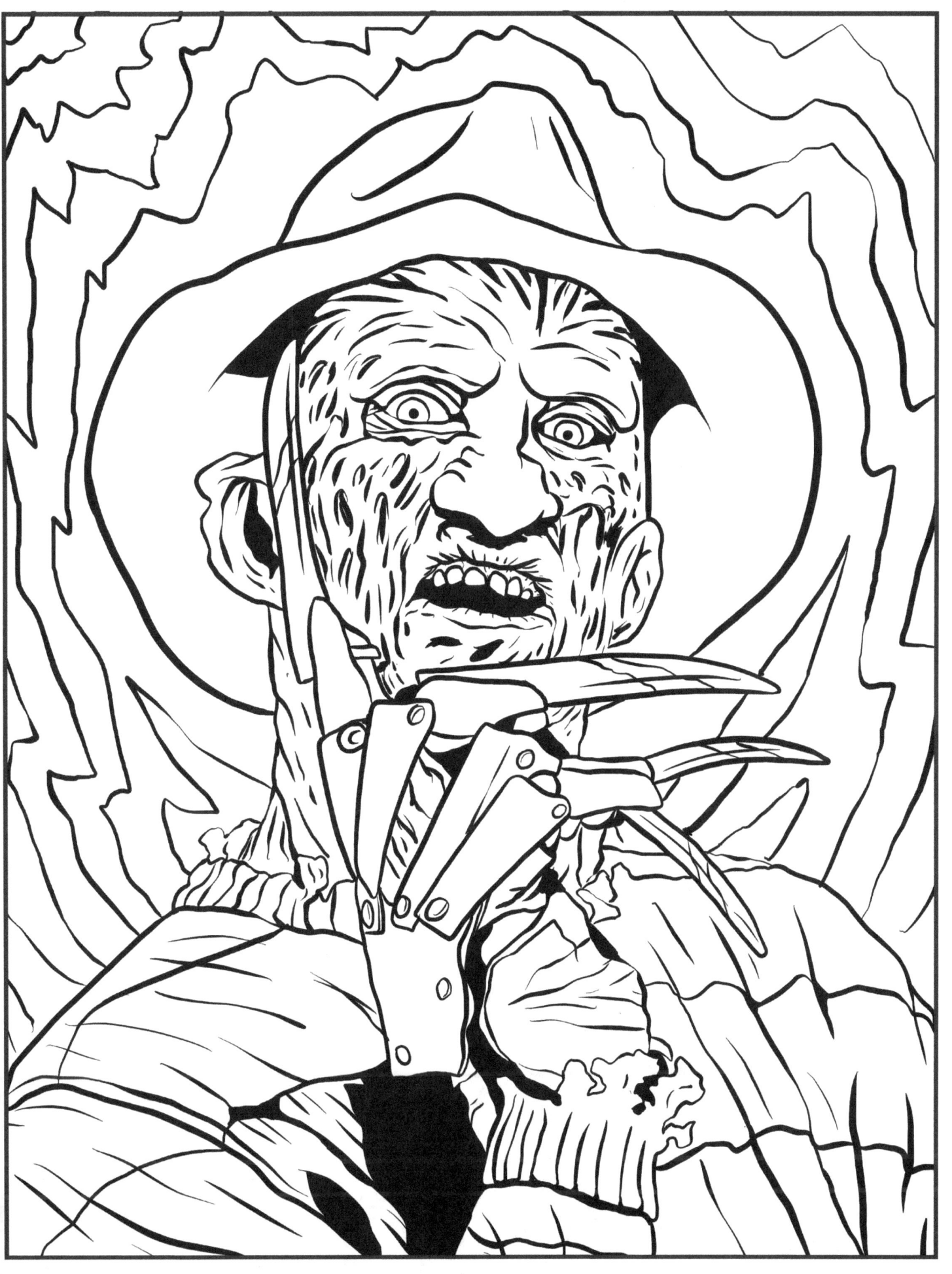

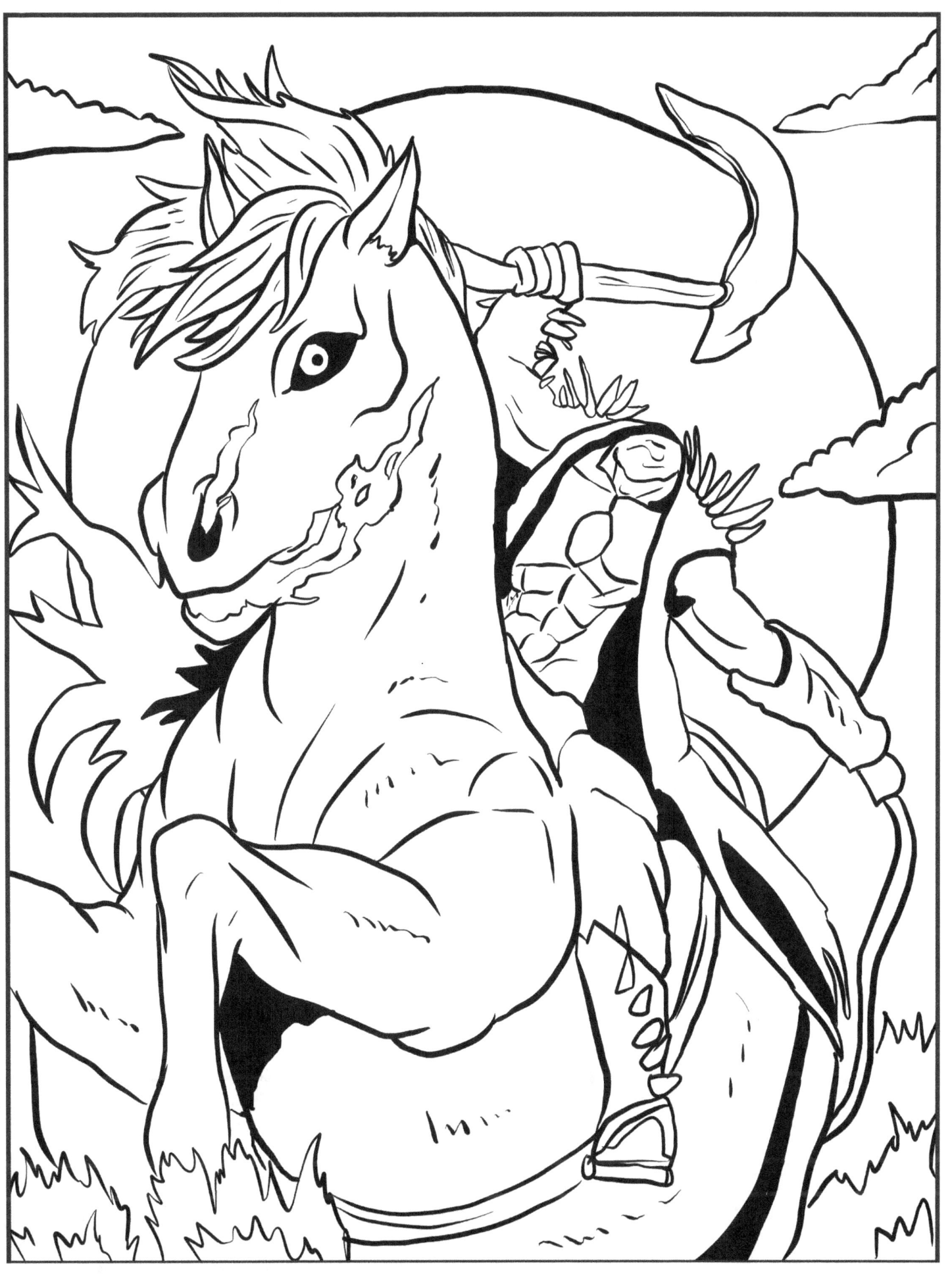

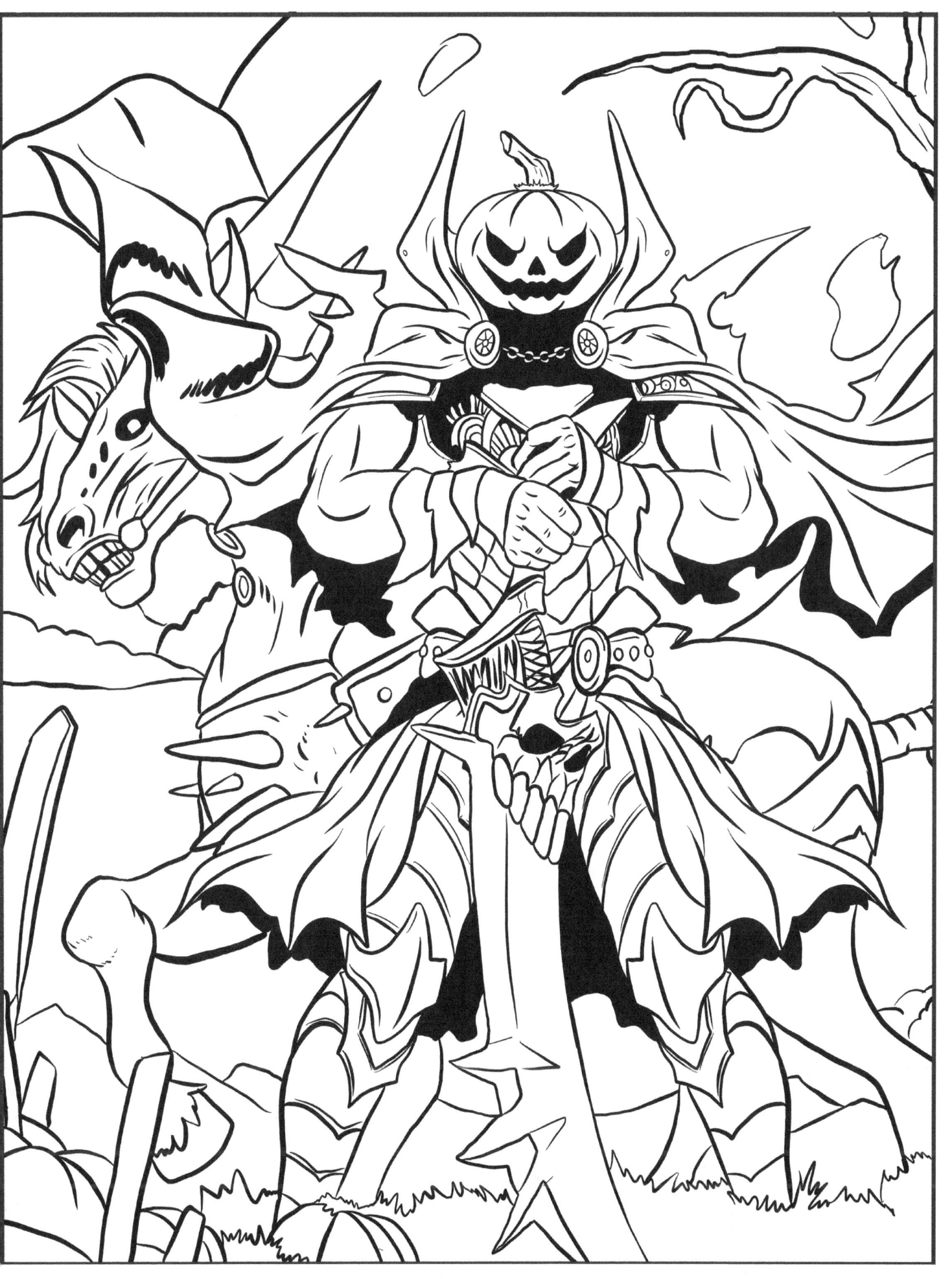

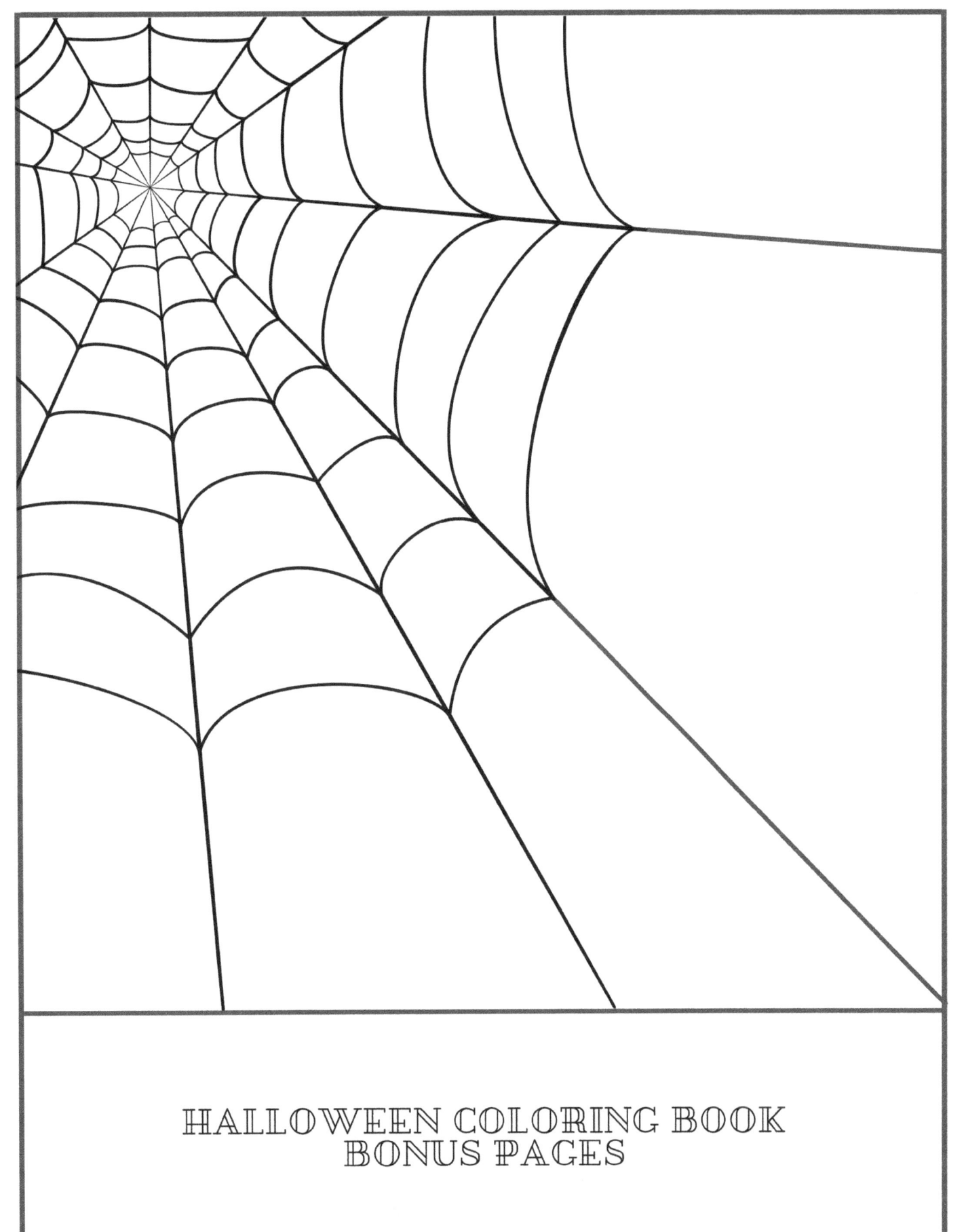

HALLOWEEN COLORING BOOK
BONUS PAGES

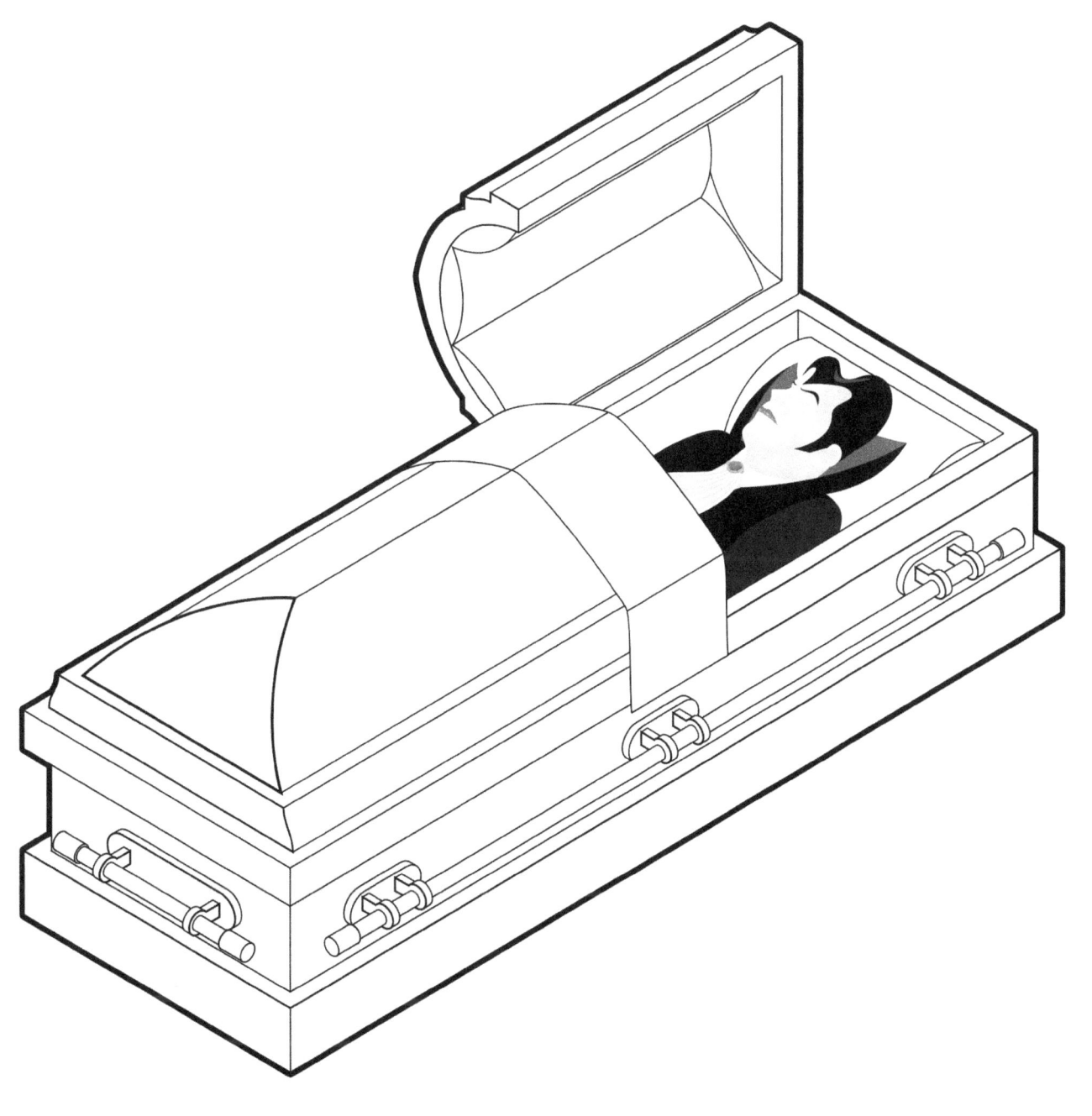

HAPPY HALLOWEEN

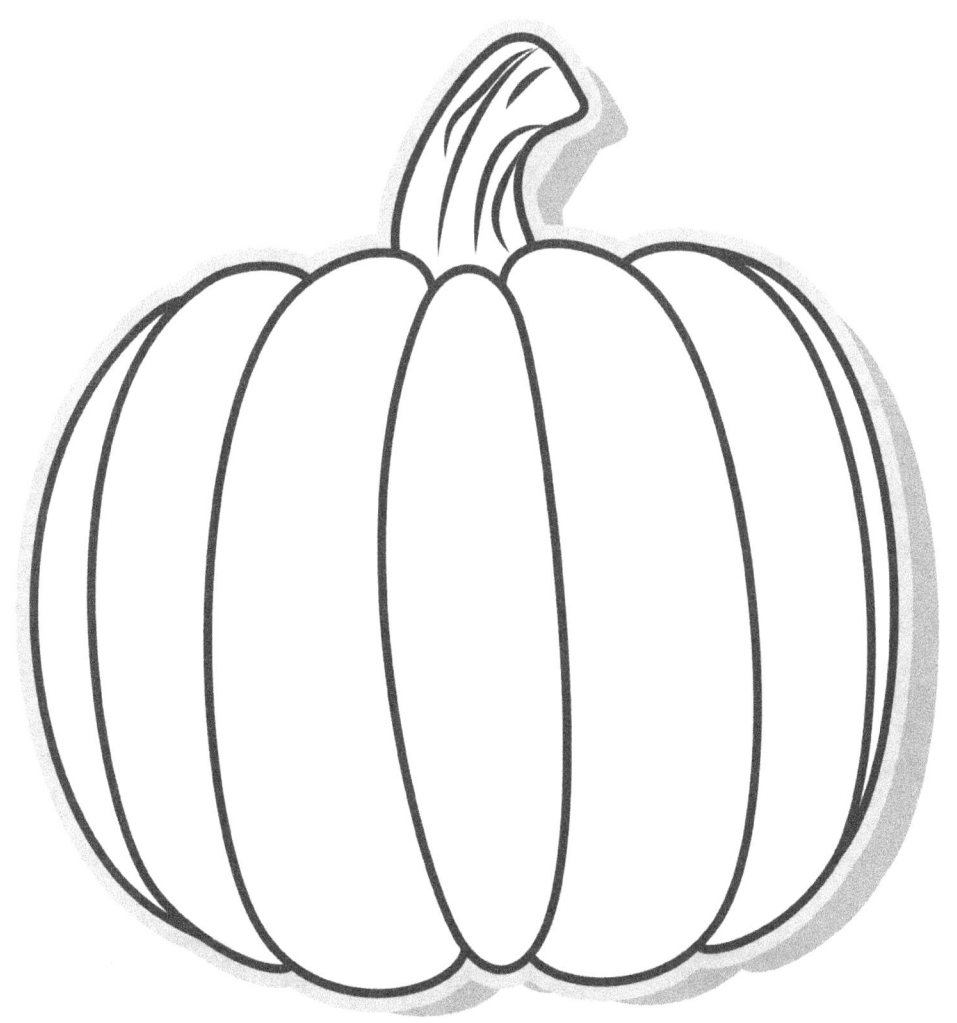

HAPPY
HALLOWEEN

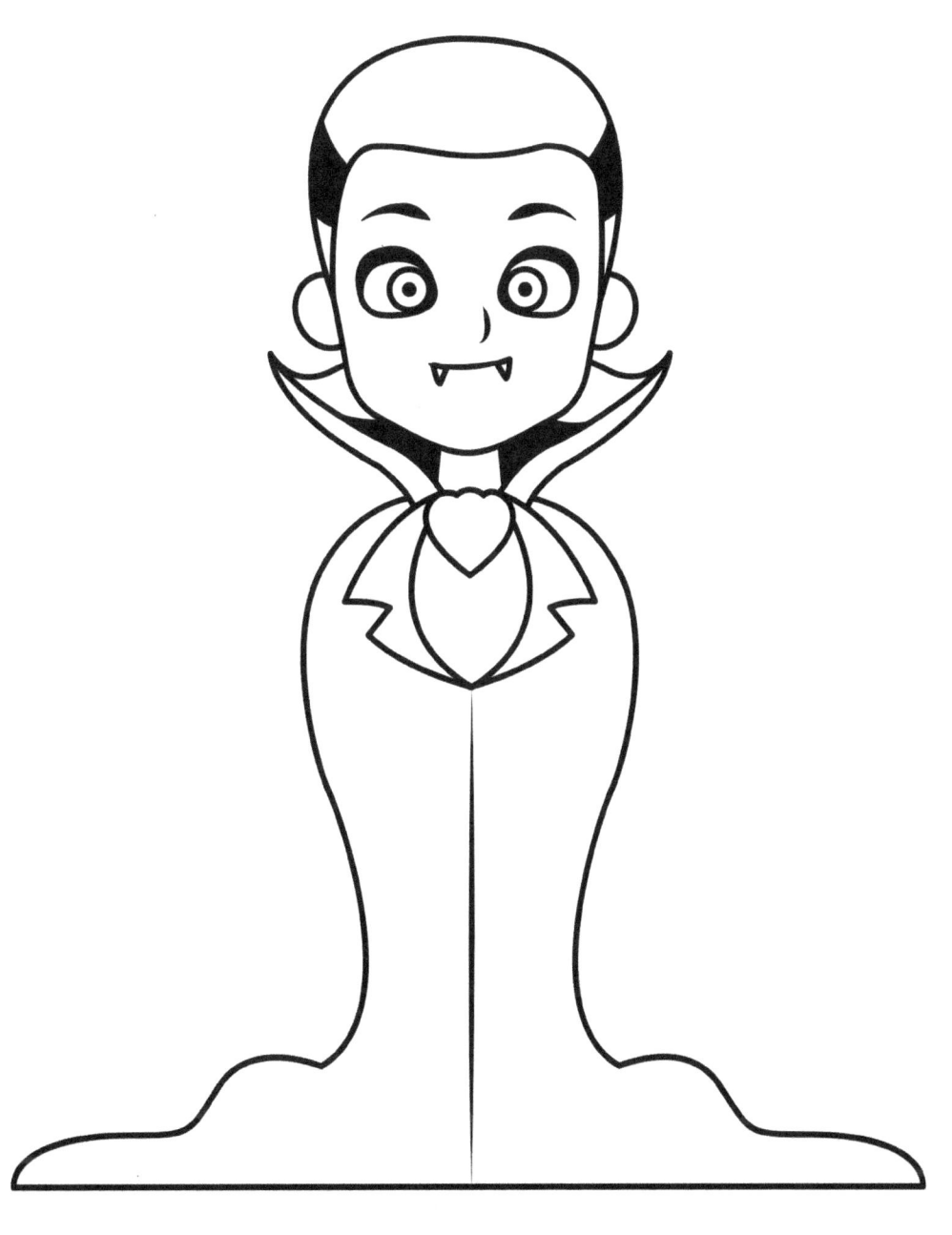

HAPPY HALLOWEEN

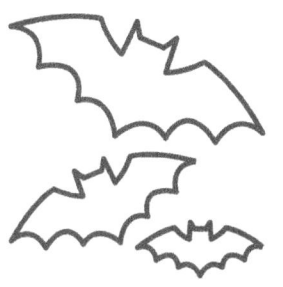
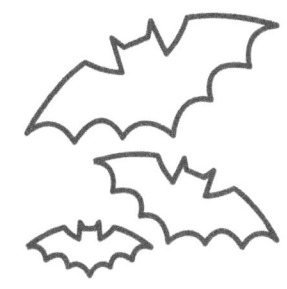
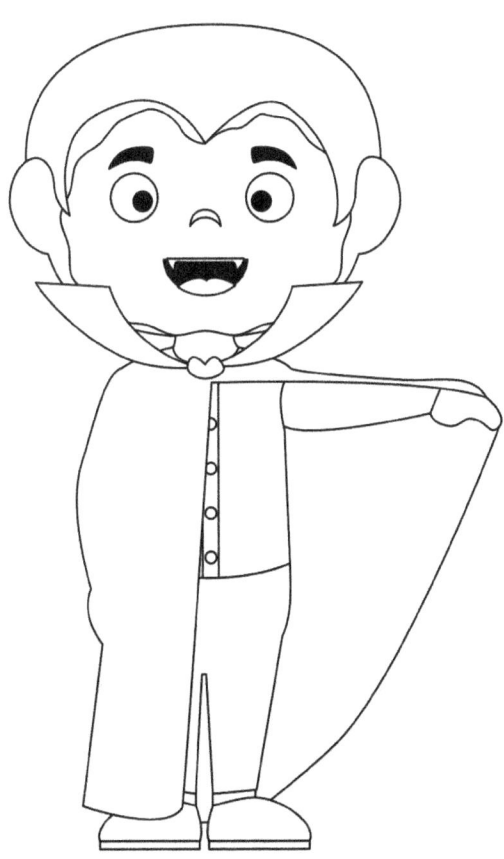
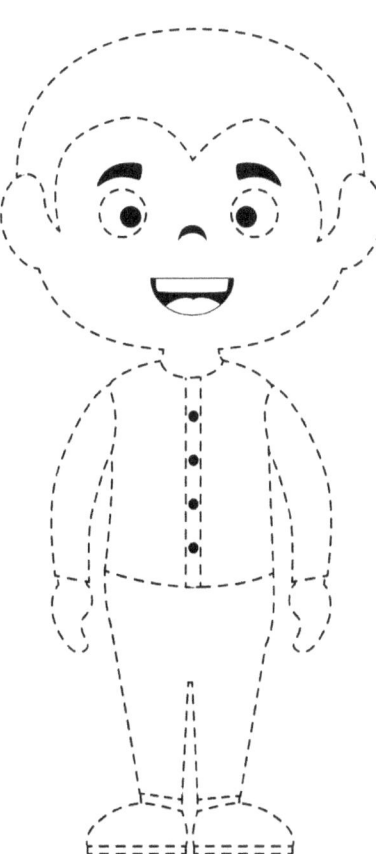

HALLOWEEN
COLORING BOOK
COLOR TEST PAGE

A small, but still super spooky, favor.

Hey there, I hope you had some fun with this coloring book and didn't get too scared with some of the illustrations. I know I certainly did when I have been coloring in my own copy!

So, I was wondering if I can call upon a little favor please? I really try hard to make good content for my coloring books so that you can experience new and exciting and fun mediums to help with your well-earned down time! An honest review is worth everything to me – I read every single one (good or bad, but I enjoy the good ones a little bit more!). So, if you could spare a few moments to give a review that would be totally awesome.

If you liked this book, I've got a few others that may be of interest to you:

Killer Cats - A Stress Relieving& Relaxation Coloring Book For Cat Loving Adults With A Sense Of Humor.
US: www.amazon.com/dp/B087SCCYM9
UK: www.amazon.co.uk/dp/B087SCCYM9

Or there's also something to help take out any anger you may be harboring deep inside:

The Curious Healing Properties of Coloring - A Cheeky but Relaxing Alternative Coloring Book for Adults.
US: www.amazon.com/dp/B089D1G9GB
UK: www.amazon.co.uk/dp/B089D1G9GB

Or something with a slightly trippy psychedelic stoner vibe:

Seriously Psychedelic - A Fun Adult Coloring Book For Relaxation & Stress Relief.
US: www.amazon.com/dp/B08DSWPT4X
UK: www.amazon.co.uk/dp/B08DSWPT4X

Or if you've got a slightly darker, twisted side to you can try this (Advance Warning – It's very 'dark' indeed):

Serial Killers Coloring Book For Adults - An A-Z of The World's Most Notorious & Deranged Male Killers.
US: www.amazon.com/dp/B08CPB7PJ5
UK: www.amazon.co.uk/dp/B08CPB7PJ5

Or, finally, if you're after something to cheer you up and give you a truly positive mindset while also bringing out your inner graffiti artist then this one's perfect:

Graffitivity - A Positivity Art Book for Relaxation & Stress Relief.
US: www.amazon.com/dp/B08GLMHMRV
UK: www.amazon.co.uk/dp/B08GLMHMRV

Thanks again and take care,   Kitty B xoxo